THE ASSERTIVE TEACHER

Dedicated to
The Education Department of Tasmania (1960–1990)
Schools of inner London (1990–1994)

The Assertive Teacher

Gwynne Wilson-Brown

arena

Published by
Arena
Ashgate Publishing Limited
Gower House
Croft Road
Aldershot
Hants GU11 3HR
England

Ashgate Publishing Company
Old Post Road
Brookfield
Vermont 05036
USA

British Library Cataloguing in Publication Data
Wilson-Brown, Gwynne
    Assertive Teacher
    I. Title
    371.11
    ISBN 1 85742 217 1 (hardback)
    1 85742 218 X (paperback)

Library of Congress Cataloging-in-Publication Data
Wilson-Brown, Gwynne, 1943–
    The assertive teacher/Gwynne Wilson-Brown.
        p.   cm.
        ISBN 1–85742–217–1 (hardback): $55.95. – ISBN 1–85742–218–X
    (pbk.): $25.95
        1. Teachers – Psychology. 2. Self-esteem. I. Title.
    LB2840.W54 1994
    371.1'001'9S – dc20   94–18300
                                                                  CIP

Typeset in 10pt Palatino by Bournemouth Colour Graphics Limited, Parkstone, Poole, Dorset. Printed in Great Britain by Hartnolls, Bodmin.

Contents

Foreword

Gwynne Wilson-Brown believes there is a world where teachers have personal power stemming from high self-esteem and open, honest behaviour. In this self-help book she shows professional teachers how to improve their self-esteem and exercise their personal rights with professional responsibility, demonstrating integrity and dignity, using true assertiveness.

Gwynne Wilson-Brown has 23 years' experience teaching in infant, primary, secondary schools and colleges, and eight years' experience in human resource development and assertion training. She has trained teachers and other professionals in the professional and personal effectiveness skills that ensure that conflict is constructive both in the areas of goal attainment and co-operative working climates. She sees much in assertiveness that contributes to the achievement of solutions where everyone is pleased.

The book goes further than merely giving skills. It takes the skills into the real world of the teacher. Case studies show how assertive language makes interactions in schools satisfying and rewarding. Men and women, primary and secondary teachers, can pursue their goals through work and maintain good relationships even when needs clash.

The skills range from asking for what is wanted to confronting unpleasantness; from helping another solve a problem to managing difficult feelings. Situations in schools which create the need for interpersonal skills are then presented as case studies, and Gwynne comments on their effectiveness. Exercises at the end of each chapter encourage the teacher to *try a new way*.

This book provides a holistic approach to human interactions in the school, whether they be with children, colleagues, or with authority.

Introduction

The social revolution taking place at the end of the twentieth century is unprecedented in history. It rivals, and probably surpasses, the speed of change experienced by those living during the Industrial Revolution. It does not help that Tofler (*Future Shock*), Handy (*The Age Of Unreason*) and other futurists gave warning; human beings generally have to undergo certain experiences before they will heed warnings and act, in advance, with a change of strategy.

The effects of this social change on education, and schooling in particular, are tremendous. No longer are children mini-adults collecting information and skills, so they can take up the place their ability and attributes, identified and certified, equip them for, in a world with empty spaces waiting to be filled. No longer do teachers have a monopoly on information. No longer are schools the only repositories of knowledge. Too often the knowledge of school contradicts the knowledge of the *real* world.

Change is a natural state for education. Compulsory schooling has been evolving for about 150 years. Teachers, although often fearing change, create, adapt and re-create in line with multiple, opposing and various objectives, recognizing cycles and balancing popular bandwagons. Change seems to be received in a pattern in three-quarters of the population:

- Denial – They can't do that.
- Anger – We'll strike.
- Bargaining – If they —, then we'll —.
- Sadness – Oh dear, poor us . . .
- Acceptance – Well, let's move on!

Such change tests the resources of teachers. The changes of the 1990s are testing the very professionalism of teachers. The status traditionally awarded

1

to those who guard knowledge and pass it to the young has been eroded.

Teachers know that the children they teach have different needs from the children they used to teach. That difference can be attributed to cultural diversification, family restructuring, unemployment, geographical mobility, new spiritualisms and ideologies. Causes and effects will keep the philosophers, psychologists and sociologists busy for eternity. Nothing will put back the way things were. Were for whom? Baroness Thatcher's Victorian values or Ken Livingstone's egalitarian Utopia? There has never been a Golden Age; that is, unless the 1950s and '60s which encouraged social mobility as a direct result of educational opportunity to the working class is recognized as such. Teachers are still attempting to create it. Today the professional status of teachers is threatened; the personal self-esteem of individuals is threatened, and the achievement of schooling itself is threatened. That threat can be an opportunity if teachers and schools can claim status from personal power rather than traditional power.

Traditional power has been under challenge since the 1940s. One of the greatest challenges came from compulsory secondary education, the Education Act of 1944. The 'adolescent' was born in school. No longer was the thirteen- or fourteen-year-old thrust into the adult world overnight with a job role as a rite of passage. Instead, the energy of the adolescent, which used to be expressed in some form of physical labour, was to be translated into mental labour. So much energy in so many young in one place! Add to this the next 20 years of cold war, nuclear vulnerability, the conquest of near space, the growth of individualism as a philosophy, and the knowledge explosion, and teacher position power has gone. The ashes of position power have been blown away by the latest reorganizations, the 1988 Education Reform Act's revolution of school management with Local Management of Schools, the National Curriculum and Performance Review. Change cannot be denied. Teachers must now claim personal power and turn the threat into an opportunity.

Power bases

The power that arises from role or position can still be seen in the dining rooms of schools where the Head can command silence, while others more lowly have difficulty, but this power is available only to a designated few or those who have it referred by proxy. The power of controlling information may still be found with a few scientific and mathematical individuals whose expertise confers expert power. Reward power is still available to the few who can bestow resources to the favoured. And the rare charismatic can still make his or her presence felt.

Today, however, teachers are required to earn their status through personal power. Each teacher is exposed to situations for which he or she is personally accountable, for example:

- A parent who challenges a teacher's professional decision.
- A governing body that can demand a set of behaviours from a professional.
- A child who can refuse to respond to a reasonable request.
- A colleague who can take unfair advantage of a situation.
- A senior who can delegate at will.
- A senior who will not delegate at a cost to the school.
- A colleague who can negotiate a better deal.
- A media reporter who can dramatize an incident.
- A system that can demand more for less.
- A system that is market economy focused.
- A system that demands personal accountability.
- A system that is different, reflecting a different world!

Change is natural and education both changes society and is changed by it. Teachers are shaped by the system and they can shape it, but to shape it they need personal power. Personal power has to be claimed. It does not come with a piece of paper and a cap and gown. It does not necessarily come with years of experience. It comes from the style of the teacher. It is skill-based and it is powered by the attitudes and values seen in the behaviour of the teacher.

Teacher style, integrity and assertion

Teachers can have many different attitudes and values. One that they share, and that draws them to teaching, is a belief in the future, the future as it will be received by the young and then created by them. They also share the belief that knowledge and skill create change, change that will be beneficial to both the individual and society. And finally, they share the belief that self-esteem is an important contributor to achievement at school.

Self-esteem is damaged whenever people disappoint themselves. They disappoint themselves whenever they do that which undermines their integrity. Integrity is a visible state. It is seen when individuals behave in line with principles to which they have publicly and privately committed themselves. It is seen when they *accept* rather than *submit* to that which is outside their control. It is possible to voice disapproval and still comply. There is no hypocrisy or double standard, but an open honesty which bears investigation. Whole schools can have integrity when the individuals in them act with integrity.

Integrity comes from acting in line with beliefs while respecting the rights of others to act in line with their beliefs. This need not produce an amoral world or a right free-for-all, where might overcomes right. It does mean a world where anyone has the right to express how in the exercising of their beliefs and rights the other is received. It does mean a belief that good overcomes bad, that abundance is more real than scarcity, that love is greater than hate. Reality is as perceived. Teachers can choose to live in a positive world or a negative one. Choosing to become assertive is choosing to live in a positive rather than a negative world where learning is necessary. This is not unacceptable to teachers who are in the business of learning; learning is dependent on communication. Communication is *the* tool of the trade and in assertive communication, the tool is shaped by openness, honesty, respect and equality. These are the ingredients of integrity; the assertive skills can both build and protect integrity.

Assertiveness is a language of integrity. It is a language of honesty, respect and equality. It can be learned. Learning anything new involves four steps:

- a time when you do not know that you do not know something
- a time when you consciously know that you do not know something
- a time when you know something when you consciously concentrate
- a time when you know something automatically.

Learning to read, cross the road, ride a bicycle involves steps. Think about a bicycle:

- 'What is a bicycle?' you say.
- It is described to you and you say, 'Ah! I see!'
- Then you see someone riding and it looks hard/easy.
- You try, and wobble a few times when you lose concentration.
- You try, and do not fall as long as you think about what you are doing.
- You ride unconsciously.

Think of learning a new language. At first you do not know there is a language called French. Then someone introduces you to it and it therefore exists for you. It might just be a name or you might hear someone speak in French and you want to do the same. It sounds good or you might have to go into a new situation where it will be useful. So your next step is to consciously learn words and phrases set by a teacher: 'Comment allez-vous?' You echo the teacher; you concentrate, but it sounds stilted and false, your accent not right. You practise and practise and then one day something clicks and you are creative with the language and it sounds real: 'Comment ça-va?' You no longer translate in your head before you utter the words.

Learning the language of assertion is like this. At first it feels strange and stilted because you are using the expressions of a *teacher*. Making it yours takes time. It is a language without 'sorry' and 'please' as punctuation marks. It reserves 'please' and 'sorry' for those occasions when you really need them. It reserves displays of anger for the rare occasions where it is appropriate and not just the explosion of an emotion. It is a language that allows caring people to care for themselves as well as for others. It is a language with no half-hearted yeses or yeses that will later be turned to noes. It is a language with no begging and no demands. It is a language of warm professionals who share their feelings and their thoughts. It is a language of integrity.

To use this language you have to accept certain rights and certain responsibilities. With the rights go responsibilities. These rights are the rights of any human being. They can be reworded ... they have the right to ... Most importantly

You have the right to forgo your rights.

Indeed, anyone who demanded their rights as due course is being non-assertive. In exercising rights, it is essential to examine each situation and be prepared to take the consequences. If these consequences always seem dire and unacceptable, then there is a need to re-examine the belief system and self-talk. If the consequences never seem scary, there may be a need to explore that inner world. Choice is the essence of assertiveness. It demonstrates flexibility, versatility without necessarily undermining consistency.

This book will show you how this language creates behaviour and operates in schools in a wide variety of situations. Case studies illuminate the theoretical points made. Chapter 1 explores the relationship between self-esteem and assertiveness, while Chapter 2 demonstrates how assertiveness is different from aggressiveness and submissiveness. Chapters 3–8 work through the main assertive skills.

KEY ISSUES

Change can be an opportunity for teachers to improve their situation.

To improve their situation teachers must communicate with integrity.

Assertiveness is a language that has integrity.

Becoming assertive involves the exercising of certain rights and responsibilities.

THE ASSERTIVE RIGHTS OF THE TEACHER

I have the right to ask for what I want without feeling guilty.

I have the right to say NO to any request without feeling guilty.

I have the right to change my mind.

I have the right to make my own decisions.

I have the right to be successful in my own way.

I have the right to privacy, solitude, and independence.

I have the right to change.

I have the right to say I do not know.

I have the right to respect.

I have the right to make mistakes.

THE ASSERTIVE RESPONSIBILITIES OF THE TEACHER

I take responsibility for my own behaviour.

I have the responsibility for carrying out those things I agreed to.

I have the responsibility for learning what I need to know.

I have the responsibility for treating others with honesty,
respect and equality.

I have responsibility for my responses to all stimuli.

I am responsible for my own successes and failures.

I take responsibility for my feelings.

I take responsibility for my decisions.

I take responsibility for allowing others enough space to be themselves.

I take responsibility for looking after myself.

1 Self-esteem and personal power

In brief

- **Self-esteem is an internal affair, a person's judgement of the private self.**
  Teachers evaluate the *self* as a result of examining the elements of self-concept which each has recorded in response to the reactions of significant people in their lives.
- **Self-esteem forms in early childhood and is difficult, but not impossible, to change.**
  Its basis is in a sense of belonging, competence and worth. Certain life events create periods of vulnerability where self-esteem can be affected, for better or worse.
- **Self-esteem is at the mercy of the inner voice.**
  Teachers listen to their inner critics and judge themselves harshly.
- **Self-esteem can be raised.**
  Self-esteem improves when teachers become more true to the *self*. Self-awareness, self-disclosure, self-acceptance and self-directed change are necessary.
- **Self-esteem affects behaviour.**
  Low self-esteem generally produces aggressive, submissive and manipulative behaviours. High self-esteem generally produces assertive behaviours.
- **High self-esteem teachers and assertive teachers have personal power.**
  Raising self-esteem enables assertiveness. Assertiveness raises self-esteem.

Self-esteem is an internal affair

Self-esteem is a gift to the self. It comes from the beliefs that teachers hold about their sense of belonging, their competence and their worth. Teachers measure their worth against some ideal that they have created. These ideals arose in early childhood when they, with children's eyes, interpreted how others they saw as important, received them. Thus children construct the pictures of their own adults as a result of their view of their physical attributes, general capabilities and performance, and personal values.

In our society, the child tends to use recognition of achievements to build the self-concept. Boys take more notice of their *doing* capabilities and girls tend to take more notice of their *being* capabilities. As the child achieves in these areas they incorporate the feedback into their self-concept, accepting or discounting the information in line with how much it is valued, at first by others and then by themselves.

For example, let's suppose a child has received and accepted the belief that reading is important, either as a deliberate message of a significant adult or as an interpretation from observation by the child. Thus the child will decide to value reading, setting a standard for 'the *best*' reader which is either achievable or not achievable. The child creates the standard of 'best' with limited information. The child, though being an excellent reader, may not reach his or her personal best and have the idea, 'I am not a good reader.' If this child does value reading, then this concept will affect the sense of worth. If this child does not value reading, then this concept will not affect the sense of worth. The self-esteem level comes from how worthy the child feels when s/he judges achievement against each personal ideal, and it is the sum total of all such self-concept evaluations. The adult continues this pattern, filtering new experiences and feedback with the child's filter, unless intervention occurs.

Case Study: Gladys, secondary deputy head, aged 45

As a child, Gladys saw how her mother hated working in a weaving mill. From birth she had been surrounded by her mother's hatred of having to go to work and leave her in care. Her mother never said this verbally. She heard her mother talk with others about how she did not belong with the mill girls who were the lowest of the low, who had no skills and were worth nothing. Her mother never said anything to her about growing up and work, but to others she said she hoped her daughter would never work like that. Then Gladys went off to school.

She heard her mother talk in admiring tones about the female teacher who dressed well, was so clever and belonged to a 'good' set of people.

Gladys decided at a young age that if she wanted her mother to admire her she would have to be like the teacher and not like the mill girls. She saw how her mother despised her father because he was unskilled and uneducated, and the message was reinforced that if she didn't want her mother to despise her she had better succeed at school.

Gladys accepted the teacher as a significant other in her life. She listened and she learned so that she came to belong to the school culture, having adopted its values. She applied what she learned so that she became competent in all her school subjects and an exemplary student. The feedback, from two teachers who had taught her unskilled father twenty years earlier, was excellent. She set a goal and defined an ideal state for herself as a learner, and became a teacher.

Gladys was never *told* that school was important, that hard work was a must, that she would be no good if she didn't succeed. Gladys, the child, taught herself all that. She set her ideal as a way to gain her mother's love, respect and admiration. From her own experience of teachers, she set the ideal of what kind of teacher was a good one. The drive to become her ideal motivated her through promotions, and, as long as she performed at a level acceptable to her, her esteem was high.

Generally, many who become teachers were children who found that school provided positive self-concept messages. Those who then valued that made it a self-esteem matter. Many of those entered the teaching profession.

Childhood, teachers, school and self-esteem

Schools are full of significant others to children, either because the parents respect the school or because the school wins the respect of the child in its own way. Having teachers who respect themselves and thus model high self-esteem is one of the greatest gifts a child can have. High self-esteem is catching.

The single most important need teachers have is for recognition, whether that be in the way of simple verbal appreciation or salary increases. Teachers need recognition from people they respect. To get it from others they have to behave as if they already have it. They have to build a *personal* power base to do this, because the *position* power base has gone.

School morale rests on the self-esteem of its teachers. As long as self-esteem is an external affair and dependent on feedback from others, it can be lowered. When self-esteem is an internal affair, it can be lifted by the individual.

As a result of their own judgements as a child, teachers continue to judge performance and decide how much worth they have, and invite people to treat them according to how much they value themselves. So the self-concept formed in childhood is confirmed or challenged in later life by most life events. There is a tendency to interpret life's events in line with the self-esteem. A person with low self-esteem will filter even good experiences and have difficulty interpreting events positively. It is not easy to lift self-esteem, but it is not impossible.

There are times when people are more open to self-esteem change because they are introspective. Adolescence and mid-life transitions are ideal times to intervene to lift the self-esteem, because at these times the self-identity is being re-evaluated. Positive experiences at these times can dramatically improve self-esteem. Crisis times, when change is forced on individuals, is another time when self-esteem is vulnerable to change. Bad times can either lift or lower self-esteem depending on how people respond to the crisis. High self-esteem people can take more crisis than low self-esteem people, whose lower supply of confidence is soon exhausted.

Teachers are caught in the middle of radical change and can take this opportunity to lift their personal self-esteem and that of the professional esteem associated with the role of teacher. 'Seize the day!' said Robin Williams in the film *Dead Poets' Society*. Some teachers are caught in personal times of stress and are vulnerable to self-esteem change, for better or worse. How you feel about the *I* indicates your degree of vulnerability. Teachers can accept responsibility for building and maintaining their self-esteem at times like these.

Every day, however, self-esteem is at the mercy of the critical self. It is affected every time a teacher reflects on a day's work. This does not mean that self-esteem is work-dependent. However, there is a tendency in Western society to tie worth to occupation. The question, 'What do you do?' generally follows on from 'Who are you?' Self-esteem should be independent of one's worth to society. The miracle of life is very special and every individual is more than any role or part they play. Yet teachers are very susceptible to confusing self-worth with ability rather than competence. Ability is related to intelligence, competence is related to sufficiency. They generally recognize children's worth as equal no matter what the ability of the child, but on themselves they are generally harder.

Self-esteem and the inner voice

Teachers tend to be their own worst critics. Inside their heads is a chatterbox ('Parent Critical' voice; see p. 109) which evaluates actions and judges against the internal ideal. Does this sound familiar?

'You should have foreseen that. You let that child get under your skin. Stupid! stupid you are, stupid you be, and stupid ever more. You don't deserve to be forgiven.

It is the voice of your own parent, echoing one heard in childhood. The chatterbox has many 'voices'.

'I said yes again and I wanted to say no. When will I ever learn? I am a passive walkover. I am incapable of standing up for myself.'

Such negative self-judgement keeps self-esteem from reaching healthy levels. It can be changed. Negative self-talk can be tackled by freezing it the minute it is detected and then positive self-judgement put in its place. Removing the chatterbox of *shoulds*, the judging element of the reflection process is a powerful way of feeding the sense of self-worth. For example,

Self 1   That was foreseeable and I did not see it. I will take note because on that occasion I did a stupid thing. I will forgive myself that foolish act and be more aware next time. I may not be perfect, but bits of me are excellent.

or

Self 2   I said yes again when I wanted to say no. Saying yes was easy there but will be hard to do later. I do not like me when I make life hard for myself. I will go now and say I have changed my mind and my answer is no.

or

Self 3   I said yes again when I wanted to say no. I said yes because I thought the repercussions of saying no would be too great. However, the repercussions of saying yes are too hard, so this is a no-win situation. I will lose this time, but next time I will remember how hard the yes is.

or

Self 4   I said yes when I wanted to say no. I did that because I thought she would be upset if I said no. I do not know that she would be upset, she could accept it and find someone who really would like to do it. I am upset. Is it better I be upset than her?

The world of the inner voice is generally outside the realm of assertion training, but it is a vital part of assertiveness. The inner critic interferes with the active part of any assertive action, and undermines the assertive rights. Being assertive with one's own inner communication is essential.

Eric Berne's[1] concept of internal voices working as parent, child and computer, as developed in his transactional analysis model, provides a starting point for getting control of these voices. Listen to the answering voices which respond to the inner question 'Where did I put that book?'

Internal answers to 'Where did I put that book?'

Parent Critical	'You are a stupid, careless dumbcluck. You should take more care. You'd lose your head if it wasn't screwed on. You probably left it in the car, and the car unlocked. When will you learn?'
Parent Rescuing	'Oh, never mind. It doesn't matter. It will turn up, or else we'll buy another.'
Parent Nurturing	'Ah well, let's not panic. We will ask around and see if anyone has seen it.'
Child Rebellious	'Oh, books have a mind of their own. Somebody must have taken it.'
Child Helpless	'Oh dear. I can't seem to find it. I lose things, please somebody help me. I cannot find it.'
Child Playful	'Oh dear. Now where did I hide that book? Naughty book. If I find you, I'll treat myself.'
Adult Computer	'I do not have the book. When did I last have it? I had it there and there and then I didn't, so it must be … in the car!'

Individuals choose voices, consciously or unconsciously, which affect their self-esteem. Putting the self down eats away at self-esteem. Catch those negative voices and treat yourself respectfully. If you think you are locked into one of the damaging responses, identify it and choose to deliberately intervene by choosing another one. The 'Adult Computer' voice is the one to use when breaking out of the damaging patterns. It is the one to use to bring others out of a highly emotional state when in an intervening position or in a confrontation. It is like the neutral gear of a car; the other voices are all 'geared' into feeling states. (See Chapter 8.) Everyone uses these voices. Sometimes, for example, it is appropriate for the teacher to choose 'Child Playful', and sometimes it is necessary to choose 'Adult Rescuing'. The uses of these will be explored later.

[1]Berne, Eric (1968), *Games People Play*, Harmondsworth: Penguin.

Realizing that choice is an option, even to the extent of not making a choice being an option, is one of the most freeing and empowering pieces of information in the world. Acting on that choice raises self-esteem. The choice doesn't have to be a perfect one; simply choosing and then acting, is enough to boost self-esteem. The status of the powerless victim goes.

Self-esteem and the teacher: external influences		
Life stage	*Significant people*	*Feedback*
Baby	Parents	What a strong grip he has! What a pretty girl!
Toddler	Family	Careful, you'll fall! Big boys don't cry!
Pre-schooler	Family	Good girls tidy up like mummy. He's such a good reader.
Pupil	Family/Teachers	You can do much better, lazy! How hard you work, good!
Student	Peers/Some adults	Good students get it right first time. You a scaredy?
Under-graduates	Tutors	I expected better of you. That's a fine achievement.
Trainee Teachers	Professionals	Well done, that was excellent. It was too difficult for you.
Teachers	Colleagues/Seniors	I never thought you could do it. You are always late.
Post Holder	Peers/Seniors	She organizes that well. Can't organize a bun fight!
Deputy	Colleagues/Seniors/ Parents	She pretends it didn't happen. He's on the ball always.
Head	Governors/ Colleagues/Parents	He's hopeless! She runs a tight ship.

Such feedback will affect the teacher when the comment is made by someone who is significant. Too often the teacher with low self-esteem gives everyone the right to evaluate him or her and accepts that feedback without evaluating it themselves. High self-esteem people accept feedback and evaluate it against their own ideal, before letting it affect them.

Raising self-esteem

Self-esteem can be lifted in many ways. Some of these are:

- Repeating positive affirmations to yourself.
- Catching the inner critic at work and halting it.
- Creating quiet and listening to your *higher* self.
- Generating positive thoughts to yourself.
- Visualizing the self you want to be.
- Writing down the things you like about yourself.
- Listing your achievements daily.
- Indulging in things you like doing.
- Doing something you have never done before.
- Examining and re-evaluating the *shoulds*.
- Examining old beliefs and either recommitting to them or replacing them.
- Setting and clarifying achievable goals.
- Not comparing yourself to others.
- Employing all your senses in the present.
- Accepting compliments.
- Forgiving yourself errors and imperfections.
- Taking risks and surviving them.
- Acquiring new personal and interpersonal skills.

All of these need a level of self-awareness. Knowing more about the self means opening up to feedback from others. (See Chapter 7.) This is risky and takes courage, but has greater impact when the individual can disclose personal feelings and own them with an 'I feel'. Telling others about the self is not a baring of the soul. It is an appropriate release of information about the self which is useful when interacting with others, because it improves relationships and makes work more effective.

Self-acceptance and self-directed change is essential; in order to develop healthy self-esteem a teacher must increase self-awareness, self-disclosure, self-acceptance and self-directed change.

Self-esteem affects behaviour

High self-esteem teachers have:

- a sense of belonging
- a sense of competence
- a belief in their essential worth

- a strong sense of identity
- expressiveness
- assertiveness
- positive relationships.

They do:

- act independently
- tolerate frustration
- accept challenges with enthusiasm
- assume responsibility
- influence others
- own and disclose their feelings honestly.

High self-esteem teachers behave assertively. Low self-esteem teachers behave non-assertively. Non-assertive behaviours include aggression, submission and manipulation. The next chapter will show how, by moving to an assertive position, teachers can lift self-esteem, and in doing so have the confidence to build personal power and act with integrity.

Increasing your self-esteem is a personal responsibility. The way you treat yourself is another person's best guide to how you want to be treated. If you value yourself, others will value you.

Exercises

1.   SELF-ESTEEM: How am I going?

I am happy	I am lazy	I am sick	I am good
I am graceful	I am a loser	I am a winner	I am a safe driver
I am OK	I am often bad	I am clumsy	I gossip a lot
I am neurotic	I teach well	I am a bore	I am a mess
I am a failure	I am a good friend	I am successful	I am sexy
I am responsible	I am a good neighbour	I am too soft	I am an angry person
I am bossy	I am clever	I am attractive	I am too passive
I make good decisions	I am not OK	I feel stressed	I should do more
I am a fool	I'm a hopeless organizer	I am enthusiastic	I am kind
I am helpful	I am not efficient	I manage time well	I procrastinate

Circle the ones that you believe about yourself.
Count the negative ones. Count the positive ones.

You now have a glimpse of your self-concept as defined by these choices. If your negatives outnumber your positives you are judging yourself harshly. No one is as hard on you as you are on yourself. Ask children to write a reference for you and check the reality of this. However, this need not affect your self-esteem. If you did not value some of the statements you identified, then they will not affect your self-esteem. Redo the exercise, underlining the circled ones that matter, and note the difference. This difference will give you an idea of your self-esteem. Concentrate on the positive things about yourself, and list the 'as I am's. Remind yourself daily of the positives about yourself.

2 Choices: aggression, submission, assertion

In brief

- **Aggressive behaviour is that which does not respect another's right to differ. It shows no respect for the other.**
  Aggressive teachers allow their feelings, particularly anger, to damage their relationships. They believe co-operation will not get them towards their goals.
- **Submissive behaviour is that which respects the other at the expense of the self. It shows no respect for the self.**
  Submissive teachers allow their feelings, particularly fear, to prevent them reaching their goals. They believe they must co-operate at the expense of their goals.
- **Manipulative behaviour is either submissive or aggressive behaviour under cover.**
  Manipulation occurs when the teacher fears being honest will not let them reach their goals or will damage relationships. They believe truth is a trade-off.
- **Assertive behaviour is that which respects another's right to be different while maintaining a respect for the self.**
  Assertive teachers manage their feelings so that they can behave with dignity and integrity. They want maximum co-operation and maximum goal achievement.
- **All teachers can choose their behaviour.**
  Teachers whose behaviour is situationally appropriate have personal power. All can behave assertively because assertion is skill-based.

THE AGGRESSIVE TEACHER

- Blasts the student for late work, refuses to mark it and tells the student to put it in the bin.
- Argues and fights loudly about having another child in the class. Does not listen to reason and is unable to negotiate a satisfactory outcome.
- Goes onto the playground duty and shouts and screams, putting maximum numbers *on the wall* (an isolated position away from other children).
- Lets everyone know that a dental appointment has had to be cancelled and gives loud notice that the new one in two weeks is on come hell or high water.
- Refuses to draw up the TV roster as his/her class does not watch TV and it should be done by someone who wants regular slots.
- Lets all the governors know before the meeting that if the money for the school trip is not forthcoming then no more out-of-school trips will ever be arranged by him/her.
- Orders the mother to hear the child read and accuses her of negligence if she does not give it priority.
- Demands the school keeper fix the door immediately and reports it to everyone who will listen.
- Spends most of life angry and justifying that anger as resulting from other people's inability to get their act together.
- Withdraws and has periods of remorse at the damage they have done.

Defining aggression

Aggression is defined as:

aggress	(v.)	to make first attack
		to intrude, to begin a quarrel
aggression	(n.)	first act of hostility
		self-assertiveness, for good or bad
aggressive	(adj.)	discourteously hostile
		offensive (with energy and initiative)
aggressiveness	(n.)	process promoting self at expense of other
		proneness to attack
aggressively	(adv.)	showing signs of emotional instability
		taking the initiative with energy

Aggressive behaviour does not respect the other

What a teacher is saying with the aggressive behaviour is:

- I am righteously angry, feel it with me.
- My needs right now are more important than anyone else's.
- Co-operation will not work.
- There is not enough to go round and I must use force to get my share.
- In order for me to win there must be a visible loser.
- Don't tackle me, you won't win.

Aggressive people pursue their goals at the expense of their relationships. Teachers, who need relationships in order to succeed in the attainment of results, cannot afford to alienate others. Being aggressive may get a result quickly but there are usually repercussions, and these repercussions may come from the aggressors themselves. Too often the aggressors are riddled with guilt when they see the hurt they may have caused, and then become meek and submissive.

Case Study: Janie, 27, primary teacher

Janie came into school on the first day of the new school year, saw that her windows had not been cleaned as she had specially requested, demanded in fact, and that the blackboard had not been painted. She went straight to the premises officer's room prepared to let him know in no uncertain terms that this was not good enough.

On the way she saw young Tom, the keeper's son, skulking in the corridor and she bawled OUT to him at the top of her voice. The child scuttered, falling over some paint pots that had been placed on the floor awaiting collection.

She arrived at the school keeper's office to find no one there. She took a piece of paper and wrote a curt note that asked what he had been doing if he had not ensured that her room was ready. She demanded he do the chores himself before the children arrived the next day.

Moving on to the staffroom, she calmed down a little, thinking a cup of tea would be nice. She opened the door and Mary, a classroom assistant, jumped guiltily and started to apologize for being there rather than delivering paint pots to the rooms. The deputy head was there and he started to ask her if she had a good break, but Janie's body language made him stop. He asked her instead what was the matter. She raised her voice to answer him and she was audible three rooms away. He listened to her complaint about the room and was starting to fill her in when she spotted the premises officer and dived out of the staffroom. The words died on his lips. He could hear her demanding an explanation from the poor man. His wife, Tom's mother, had died during the holiday break.

Janie was angry that her room was not as it should be. Janie was angry with her father for leaving her mother, angry at her sister for having a baby and bringing it home for her mother and Janie to look after. She didn't know she was angry. She thought she was definite and precise, a person who called a spade a spade. It did not register with her that others saw her with trepidation, that they feared to hold any different opinion from hers. She thought other people should be like her. She would do what she had said she would do.

Her self-awareness was blinkered, tied to her own inner world. She did not read the feedback from the body language of those with whom she had interactions. She had fought to the bitter end and sometimes won and sometimes lost in interaction with other *strong-minded* people. She had trampled the *weak-minded* underfoot. She had not met an assertive person who would honestly and non-judgementally describe how she was being received right there and then.

Only an assertive person could manage Janie both short- and long-term. An assertive person would choose a time when Janie was in listening mode and describe to her, without blaming Janie, how her behaviour affected others.

In reality there can be many aggressive outbursts and their effects are usually short-term. Reducing these is possible and beneficial to all who work in schools. However, when schools have aggressive personalities on the staff who can dominate and wound others, even unintentionally, they are unhappy places. Wounded teachers react with fight-or-flight behaviours and a lot of winning and losing goes on. Stress levels go up, teachers burn out and the educational programme suffers.

THE SUBMISSIVE TEACHER

- Accepts late work from the student, even though it is the student's pattern to be late and all the other work is marked.
- Sighs in the staffroom about being given another pupil and having to squeeze in another desk to accommodate her.
- Does the playground duty and misses the dental appointment she has waited weeks for and earns the sympathy of colleagues.
- Makes excuses to the Head for not having drawn up the roster for TV allocations as requested. Promises to do so soon.
- Doesn't attend the governors' meeting to present the case for trip finance, because of illness. Hopes the Head will present the case.
- Doesn't ask the parent to hear the child read but says she will hear the child at lunch time.
- Hopes the school keeper will notice the difficult door and mend it. Might drop hints after a few days.
- Spends most of life doing things s/he doesn't want to do. Often despairs of all the things that need doing and don't get done. Wishes people would care more. Feels tired a lot of the time.
- Has occasional outbursts of 'It's not fair' and lashes out before breaking down. Has a few health problems.

Defining submission

Submission is defined as:

submit	(v.)	to yield, resign, to lay down
		to refer for decision-making, sanction
submission	(n.)	an act of surrender
		a respectful contention
submissive	(adj.)	willing to consent
		ready to yield or comply
submissiveness	(n.)	process of resigning respectfully
		process of subordinating the self
submissively	(adv.)	acting resignedly
		behaving subdued and low-toned.

Submissive behaviour does not respect the self

What a teacher is saying with submissive behaviour is:

- I am a nice person, see how I defer to you.
- My needs are not as important as yours.
- Co-operation will not work.
- There is not enough to go around and I will do without.
- In order for you to accept me I must lose.
- Nothing is worth a fuss.

Submissive people give up their goals in favour of relationships. Teachers who give up their goals do not achieve their objectives and work satisfaction is low. Being submissive may get a person out of a situation with minimum unpleasantness, but there is an aftermath that has to be endured. Too often the submissive person transfers anger to a scapegoat or becomes ill.

Case Study: Pelle, 36, primary teacher

Pelle was the only man on the staff of 22 apart from the premises officer. He had been given year 4, a group of 34 pupils, seven of them statemented. The Head had asked him if he could cope with this difficult class and he hadn't liked to say he dreaded it. It was now seven weeks into autumn term and he did not think he could get to Christmas. It was Friday morning break and he was on duty in the playground. The mother of Barrie, one of his previous year's class, entered the yard and approached him. She said her son, now in first year at secondary school, was having a lot of trouble and she wondered if he would stay after school one night per week and talk with him until things were sorted out.

Pelle didn't like to refuse. The mother would be upset. The Head would be disappointed in him. The boy was a nice kid. His teacher would have done it for him in similar circumstances, he was sure. He could think of no good reason for saying no. So he said yes, and agreed on Tuesdays at 4 p.m.

Tuesday arrived and Pelle was stretched to his limit by the class. He avoided exploding all afternoon and escaped to the staffroom for a cup of tea. The thought of Barrie arriving at 4 p.m. was too much. Could he escape, just forget? Could he explain to the Head and ask him to deal with it? No, he could not. The ideal Pelle would cope.

Whether Pelle would be a help to the ex-student is debatable. In doing so he is stretching himself so far that his *real* work, and his own health, will suffer. Submitting to all requests because he cannot say no, believes he should not say no, shows that Pelle cannot distinguish the important from the not-so-important. The important issues will suffer because he cannot resource them sufficiently. He does not demonstrate competence in this area.

Pelle is not sufficiently self-aware to see how his behaviour is hurting him. His expectations of himself are unreal. He believes the other person's needs are greater than his own, and he does not value himself. Pelle is not even free of the requests of assertive people who would expect an honest no from him if he felt a no was appropriate. Barrie's mother was assertive. She had alternatives if Pelle said no. Becoming assertive will allow Pelle to say no or set limits, and begin to prioritize and plan for the effective use of his time, energy and talents.

When schools have submissive teachers in them, relationships appear to be conflict-free. However, the goals of the school are not being achieved, because everyone is concentrating on keeping harmony because they falsely believe non-compliance will be unpleasant. When submissiveness hides conflict, the emotional turmoil is beneath the surface. Then trouble explodes over some triviality that is the final straw and everyone is bruised.

Submissiveness can be an excuse for not achieving goals. When teachers can prove that they had too much to do, they can excuse a lack of excellence. Or, the submissive ones develop somatic illnesses that create spaces for them and set boundaries. Assertive people are rarely ill.

Teachers generally submit to authority because they feel they have no choice. They deny their own authority, their professional integrity.

The manipulative teacher acts under cover

The manipulative person can appear to be submissive, aggressive or assertive. The receiver of manipulation feels conned some time after an interaction with a manipulator.

Case Study: Frank, 27, history teacher

Frank was a good-looking, charming, polite young man with intelligence and a quick wit. He was popular with his Head and seniors, but his colleagues were wary of him.

One day, Sylvia, a history colleague, was desperate for someone to relieve her 15 minutes early for lunch so that she would have time to go to the bank to sort out a problem. She knew Frank was free that period and asked him if he could take her class for the last 15 minutes. In his charming manner, he agreed and asked her to photocopy some sheets he would need in the afternoon. She did these in her recess break.

12:05 arrived and Frank had been due at noon. A child arrived with a message that Frank had to cover for a sick teacher and could not relieve her. Sylvia did not get to the bank and incurred a hefty overdraft fee. She was very angry with Frank. Later that day Frank apologized and said he had been unable to relieve her because of the surprise cover. She accepted the excuse but felt uneasy somehow.

Next day, she learned that Frank could have explained to the deputy that he was relieving her at noon and the deputy would have found someone else without a problem. Frank had not been assertive with the deputy and seen through his commitment to her.

Frank looked after Frank: when a senior was to be impressed all else had to give way because Frank wanted to be seen favourably. There are many Franks. A truly assertive Frank would have openly told the deputy of the responsibility he had to Sylvia and worked it out with the deputy.

THE ASSERTIVE TEACHER

- Has an upright body posture that is calm and in charge.
- Uses eye contact to build trust and disarm aggression.
- Gives *I* messages which personalize thoughts and feelings.
- Asks for what is wanted honestly.
- Listens in silence until another has finished.
- Always speaks with respect for the other in voice and body.
- Sees/listens and speaks in a ratio of 4:1.
- Does not allow the mood or behaviour of another to determine theirs.
- Sets limits on what is expected of them.
- Says no to a request and yes to the person.
- Meets aggression with words which show they receive the feeling of the other.
- Receives criticism without necessarily accepting it as true.
- Uses 'broken record' repetition in response to unreasonable requests.
- Helps others appropriate to their need.
- Enables others to solve their own problems by focusing them on their solutions.
- Pre-empts unwanted requests with a request not to be asked.
- Challenges unpleasantness like put-downs.
- Uses negative enquiry and negative response to uncover real issues.
- Meets their own needs with the help of others.
- Asks for back-up when issues are beyond their management.
- Chooses to be aggressive or submissive if and when a situation warrants it.

Defining assertion

Assertion is defined as:

assert	(v.)	to vindicate or defend by argument
		to lay claim to, to declare strongly
assertion	(n.)	an affirmation
		the act of claiming one's rights
assertive	(adj.)	confirming confidently
		positive (dogmatic)
assertiveness	(n.)	a process of affirming
		a way of acting positively
assertively	(adv.)	doing something positively
		acting with confidence.

Assertive behaviour respects the other as well as the self

What a teacher is saying with assertive behaviour is:

- I respect myself and I respect you.
- Our needs are equally important.
- Co-operation will work for both of us.
- There is enough for everybody.
- Everyone can win.
- Let's work it out together.

Assertive people believe goals and relationships are of equal importance and they spend time and energy on creating satisfying outcomes and interactions. They do not think or feel that difference and confrontation need be unpleasant. They know that time and energy will have to be found to resource win-win solutions and that they can choose aggression or submission when time and energy are short.

Assertive teachers act on the understanding that all people are equal, no matter what role they are in. They recognize and respect the human being in any role: pupil, student, parent, colleague, support staff, governor, senior or interested other. Assertive teachers can act like this because they claim their rights and accept their responsibilities realistically. They have a sound knowledge base and are clear about their personal and professional objectives.

Assertiveness is skill-based

In order to be assertive, teachers must have personal competence in:

- speaking openly and honestly
- listening actively
- avoiding gate-slamming communications
- facilitating door-opening communications
- managing their emotions
- setting limits on what is expected of them
- knowing when to counsel and when to confront
- negotiating for what they want
- recognizing problem ownership
- using no-lose management strategies
- managing value collisions.

Can teachers be so competent? Yes. Competence is based on skills which can be learned by a cumulative process which supports skills becoming behaviours. The process is reflective, adaptive and synergistic, and feelings as well as thoughts are dealt with.

Assertive teachers can operate in any school, under any management style. If the school is very formal, conservative, tradition-bound or totalitarian with autocratic leadership that denies consultation, the assertive teacher can accept the boundaries and work within them, confronting with genuine honesty if personal philosophies create conflict. If the school is very informal, liberal, responsive and individualistic with *laissez-faire* leadership that provides little policy and decision-making, the assertive teacher can define the standards with genuine interactions.

Aggressive and submissive people have their own ways of resisting assertive people. Other people can not be changed with assertiveness, but when receiving assertive behaviour, many people see its advantages and choose it.

THE BENEFITS OF ASSERTIVENESS

- Getting more of what you want.
- Getting less of what you don't want.
- Expressing your feelings and not storing them up as stress.
- Being true to yourself and consequently being happier.
- Having good relationships with all kinds of people.
- Having a way of doing the job that is satisfying.

THE COSTS OF ASSERTIVENESS

- Spending a lot of time and energy at first.
- Taking risks because of revealing feelings and some weaknesses.
- Increased vulnerability to being taken advantage of.
- Alienating others who are jealous or threatened by your success.
- Accepting increased self-awareness.
- Being responsible for who you are and what you do.

Case Study: Anna, 49, further education tutor

Last week Anna arrived to teach her assertion class at a college where she had been teaching part-time for three years. The room she had been allocated was in the process of being redecorated and the previous week she and the class had tolerated wet paint smells because no other room was available. On checking with administration before leaving, she had been assured that all would be well the next week. This week, carpet was being laid and all the furniture had been removed. She, with the class as audience, approached the administration officer and asked where she should take her lesson. The administration officer said she would have to find another room for herself if there was no furniture there, because no other room was available on the chart. The conversation went like this:

Anna   I cannot do that. Last week we lost 20 minutes of the lesson because of trying to find an alternative room and so I checked that the room would be ready. I do not want our learning time used this way. I need another solution.
Officer   There isn't another solution.
Anna   Will you please check to see if there is another room?
Officer   There isn't, I know.
Anna   My problem is the time that is being wasted. I would like you to find the keeper and have him set up the room. It is your responsibility to have a room ready for us while I do the register here in the foyer.
Officer   I don't know where he is.
Anna   Please find him and tell us when the room is ready.
Officer   I cannot leave the desk.
Anna   We will keep an eye on the desk while you search.
Officer   Here he is. Anna wants you to put her furniture in G11.
Keeper   But I won't be here to lift it out again for the carpet layers.
Anna   That is a lower priority problem. Right now I have 17 students

	who have paid for a lesson they are not getting. The priority is customer satisfaction.
Officer	Do it!
Keeper	The bar of the theatre is empty. Why don't they go there?
Anna	My priority is a classroom. Will you please ensure that this problem does not happen next week.

The officer had felt attacked, either because she felt guilty at not having the room ready or because she was used to people accepting her authoritative orders. The feelings were hers. Anna felt she had to demonstrate to the class that calm reasonableness would win, even if time was lost. A solution arrived, outside those envisaged possible.

The next week the room was still the same and a different administration officer was in charge.

Anna	My room is not ready for the third week running and we have lost a lot of teaching time. I feel very angry with myself and with college administration. Perhaps I should have rung the Head of Centre to check and perhaps the keeper should have checked. I need a room now.
Officer	What did you do last week?
Anna	Most unsatisfactory, but we worked in the bar area of the theatre.
Officer	There is a group there but I can move them onto the stage because they do not need to sit. Come with me.

This solution was still unsatisfactory and Anna would have to contact 'higher-ups' to ensure the problem was resolved. She rang and talked with the Head of Centre who told her the room had been done so that an outside business group could use it at a high rental and that it was not available for her assertion class anymore. So Anna asked what arrangements had been made for her class.

Head	Well, you only have three sessions left. Can you manage in the theatre bar until the end of term?
Anna	No, that is unacceptable. My students deserve a learning space that assists their learning. We have accommodated the college's problem for three weeks and we want a proper room for the rest of term.
Head	Leave it with me and I'll get back to you.
Anna	I will ring you tomorrow at three to see what has been decided.

Anna does ring, again and again. She knows that persistence is essential, particularly if she is to establish herself as someone who can reasonably pursue an issue to a satisfactory conclusion. She may have to settle for the theatre bar. In the short term, she may lose. In the long term, however, she knows that as long as she respects herself and her *opponent*, she will have a suitable room. Albeit next year!

What can be learned about assertiveness from this exchange? Assertion can be used by the powerless to get what they want or, at the very least, let the powerless one know that every resource available has been used. Powerlessness comes from believing that there are no choices and no processes to use. Those with greater power can still abuse the powerless but the less powerful keep their self-respect and do not destroy themselves with inner, critical condemnation.

Would aggression have got a better result? Or immediate capitulation? There might be occasions when the answer to these would be yes. The assertive person decides; it is the element of choice that makes assertiveness so self-affirming. The teacher can choose to be aggressive, submissive, assertive – an assertive teacher who has some control over feelings can choose. This does not mean that assertive teachers have less feeling or no feeling at all. Assertive teachers feel and *describe* those feelings in what they say to the other. Non-assertive teachers do not control those feelings, they either *show* them and let feelings dictate what they do next, or hide them and suffer later.

There are many ways of responding to events. Imagine the door swinging onto a teacher because a student had let it go. A teacher might call, 'Stupid girl!', or 'Stupid me, I should have anticipated that', or 'Oh, that scared me. When you let the door go, it swung dangerously at me.' There *is* a choice. Having made an initial submissive response, however, it is not necessary to stick with it. What must be avoided is a swing to the opposite extreme, aggression. Sadly this is what occurs with both submissive and aggressive responses. Aggressive teachers suddenly see the effect of their aggression, feel remorseful and become very submissive for a while. Submissive teachers suddenly experience the last straw (however trivial) and explode aggressively. It is possible and advisable to work through a series of gradually intensifying responses. Imagine a child starting to get on the nerves of a teacher:

Intensity 0　Ignoring disruption.
Intensity 1　A dirty look and a sigh.
Intensity 2　Please do not talk when I am talking.
Intensity 3　I am serious. Your talking must stop because it is disruptive.
Intensity 4　If you do not stop talking when I am teaching then I must discipline you. (The assertive teacher has an appropriate different strategy for each child.)

Intensity 5   I am very angry now. You can see the deputy at playtime.
Aggression   That's it, you stupid, noisy, good-for-nothing kid. You spoil
it for everybody. Off you go!

Note the step-by-step movement from first to third person, to description of a tangible effect, to gradual insistence, to a move to position power, to, finally, a threat being made and carried out. You might think that a child will take advantage of this sliding scale of responses. True. You have to know that they will and you must choose which level to start on. Many teachers may say the child deserves an earful. Fine! Do it! But do not say you were too assertive. *Choose* to respond aggressively. Remember that the swing from submission to aggression results in the charge of unfairness and alienates whole groups of children, whom you then have to win back. Adults are no different.

THE ASSERTIVE TEACHER

Asks for what he wants
I want the primary helper on Tuesday mornings.

Uses I rather than you messages
I cannot see any truth in what you are saying.

Says no to what she doesn't want
I do not want to do that today.

Sets limits on what is expected of him
I cannot do it that way. I will contribute in another way.

Delivers praise and criticism that is specific
I liked the way you presented that argument.
I did not follow your line of argument about poverty being unavoidable.

Receives praise and criticism with dignity
I appreciate your kind words.
It is true that I am late today by six minutes.

Helps by enabling another to handle a problem
I see your quandary. How do think a first line of attack should go?

Counters aggression with a calm
I see your anger and it is making you unreasonable. I will come back later.

> *States own feelings honestly*
> I feel both disappointed and frustrated by your decision.
>
> *Confronts the difficult*
> This is not easy for me. We must address this before it becomes impossible.

Assertive teachers behave in ways that demonstrate self-respect and honesty. They do not take short cuts where integrity is at stake, but instead explore and challenge their attitudes, beliefs and values. They make time available for sorting out processes that promote good relationships and the appreciation of diversity. After rehearsing new skill behaviours in feedback situations, assertive teachers take calculated risks in the school world. These risks involve accepting imperfections, but promote an atmosphere of equality and a lack of victimization.

Exercises

1. Identify how you would respond aggressively, submissively and assertively to each of the following situations:

    *   Someone pushes in front of you in the staffroom morning tea queue.
    *   A work colleague rings you at midnight with a request.
    *   The Head asks you to cover playground for an absent staff member.
    *   Your pay does not go in the bank and you are overdrawn.
    *   An adolescent flings his/her school bag at your feet and you trip.

    What would be the advantage and disadvantage of each response?

2. Observe the behaviour of others:

    *   Look for aggressive behaviours.
    *   Look for submissive behaviours.

    What do people get out of behaving this way?

3 Asking for what you want

In brief

- **95% of what people want can be had for the asking.**
  Teachers who know what they want, ask the right person at the right time in the right way to gain what they want.
- **The asking must be done appropriately.**
  Teachers can work out what they want as visible goals, use active voice, plan how to ask and have contingency plans, rehearse, and then say thank you for the request being received.
- **Goals must be realistic and achievable.**
  Teachers must identify what they want as specifics and make an achievement plan.
- **A No response can be accommodated.**
  Teachers who ask are not destroyed when their request is unsuccessful.

Knowing what you want

It is a simple fact that some people get a lot of what they want. Most of what people want can be had for the asking. This is as true at work as it is in everyday life. It is true for teachers as well as other professionals. Teachers generally do not ask because they do not know what they want, who to ask, how to ask, and they do not believe they have the right to ask.

When teachers identify what it is they want, their chances of getting it are doubled. Add to this, knowing who to ask, how to ask and believing what they want is OK, and a successful outcome becomes the norm. This builds confidence, self-esteem, and a sense of personal control or power. Work satisfaction is an outcome.

Some of the things that teachers want are: a fair go, a government that will fund according to need, respect for professionalism, a respite from media criticism, and decent-size classes. These are idealistic, ambiguous, abstract goals that need whole strategies to support them, but they can be worked towards once the elements that compose them are identified as achievable, recognizable, concrete outcomes. Asking for a fair go, specific funds, respect and a respite from criticism, etc., must be practised in everyday life before teachers can successfully request a system to accommodate their needs. Teaching pupils to walk before teaching them to run is something teachers know well. The same principle must be applied to teachers themselves.

The process of learning to identify what you want as a recognizable outcome is a first skill. This process might include:

- I do not know that I want anything.
- I do know that there is something I want.
- I do want a class size I can manage.
- I can manage any size class with the right support.

Some non-assertive teachers, however, would rather moan than have things how they want them. Their need for sympathetic appreciation is often greater than the need for successful outcomes. This chapter is about moving towards successful outcomes.

Asking appropriately

Asking involves a series of steps. If teachers are to get what they want they must develop the ability to set concrete goals, communicate with *I* messages and be prepared to plan and rehearse. Finally, teachers must be able and willing to *move* and negotiate.

- *Have visible goal targets*

For example, the goal of having a better classroom may involve a change of room or improvements like having the door lock fixed, having a carpet square laid or having the windows cleaned.

- *Ask in an active voice*

The request must be made in an obvious active voice – I want, rather than the passive 'It would be a good idea if ...' or 'Don't you think it would ....'

- *Have a plan with a series of contingency options*

Rehearse and visualize the best, tolerable and worst responses to your request. Have a number of options built into your plans. Great innovators have asked the question, 'If it is impossible, what does it need to make it possible?' Jasmin's story, below, demonstrates the steps towards achieving positive changes.

Case Study: Jasmin, 45, primary teacher

Jasmin is tired and unmotivated, and it is still only the start of term. Her class has five statemented children and has not settled into quiet working patterns after four weeks, the classroom itself badly needs some aesthetic work and she has an irrational desire to not do playground duty on Fridays, as timetabled. It is all too much; she fears she'll never get through the year. Part of her wants to give it all up as too hard, part of her wants to rebel and create chaos, and a third part wants a work situation that is rewarding. She identifies her wants:

  a quiet class
  progress for her pupils
  some new ways of handling children with special behavioural problems
  some new ways of creating learning for statemented children
  her classroom improved
  more control over her daily life.

What can she do? Her options are limited only by her imagination. Here are some of them:

  resign in the belief that all is hopeless – physically submissive flight
  stop caring and just draw her pay – mentally submissive flight
  create a fuss and refuse to teach until . . . – totally aggressive fight
  go public, moan to parents and press – totally aggressive fight
  grumble her way and take sickies – fighting flight
  identify actions which will make life better – assertive planning.

Some options are better than others for her and the school. An assertive Jasmin will want to achieve her goals without causing hardship for others. This is the guiding principle when deciding what she wants. Does she want sympathy? Then a moaning course, either verbally or by body language, is, in the short term, best. She will at first get sympathy, but this will quickly vanish as she gets a reputation as a moaner. Does she want to make others *hop*? Then an angry tirade, either at the decision-makers or by scapegoating, will, in the short term, get some action. But will she gain a reputation as a stirrer and quickly alienate people who could help her? Does she want to get on with her job, with rewards in job satisfaction and pay? Then an assertive choice will give her short-term satisfaction and long-term success.

Jasmin chose to have real outcomes and so to be assertive. It will require a high initial investment of energy from her, but she will save on the constant energy which she will need if she faces the world with aggression or absorbs the pressure inwards submissively. She does want to stay teaching for many different reasons, some of them professional (she can be good at it) and some of them personal (she has a big mortgage and her pay is good).

Goals must be realistic and achievable

Jasmin must identify a series of things she wants that are achievable, realistic and concrete. She has accepted as fact that people around her have it within their power to accede to her requests, and she has accepted that she has the right to ask. If she had asked for a new room, some different children and three full-time support staff, her goals would have been unachievable, unrealistic and rather abstract. If she had asked for recognition that her burdens were huge, she might have felt temporarily good but that would not have improved her situation.

Jasmin has taken one specific thing she can move towards to get what she wants, from each of her generalist list of wants. These include:

> one of the constant talkers is not to talk while she is teaching
> to go to a conflict management seminar in school time
> funds from the governing body for a museum trip
> a parent to hear her own child read every night
> her classroom door mended
> to not do playground duty on Fridays.

Now that she has moved from the general to the particular, she must plan how she will make it happen.

Jasmin and the constant talker

First, Jasmine maps out the steps of achieving her goal:

What is wanted?	No talking while she is teaching.
Who is to be asked?	One pupil, Billie, not easy, not hard.
Can the pupil do it?	Yes, already does it in assembly.
What is pupil's viewpoint?	Teacher's boring, I must tell my friend.
How is pupil to be asked?	When alone, in dialogue with pupil

	contribution to answer.
Plan:	What is wanted from pupil?
	best: silence when teacher talks;
	worst: 50% less talking.
Rehearse:	Write script and role-play:
	teacher as pupil;
	friend as teacher.

Mentally envisage a number of scenarios. Think through worst/best:

                                 pupil rebellious

                                 pupil passive

                                 pupil eager to comply.

Do It!

Evaluate and adapt:	Redo it another way with pupil; adapt for use with another pupil.
It could go like this:	(Use the specific 'I'.)

After going through the preliminary steps, Jasmin has her conversation with Billie. Her tone is genuine because Jasmin believes in equality, even with a child.

Jasmin	Billie, I think we should have a talk. 1:20 p.m. will be a good time for both of us today. I will come to collect you from play. [Note the non-negotiable timing; teacher defines the situation because she owns the problem.]
Billie	Oh, miss!

At 1:25, having collected Billie, Jasmin takes him to the classroom.

Jasmin	Billie, I wanted us to talk about how we work together. My job is to help all the pupils in my class to learn all the things they need to do. It is hard to do that for 32 different pupils. I have to ask all of you sometimes to be silent and listen to me so that I do not have to say the same things over and over again. I need you to be silent at those times. What do you think? [This invites the child to problem-solve.]
Billie	(Is silent.)
Jasmin	Billie. [The persistent use of his name focuses Billie on himself.] Will you help me? [Very few children under 12 can resist this.]
Billie	It's not me, miss. It's Kati.
Jasmin	Sometimes it is Kati and sometimes it is you. [The teacher agrees with child.] I want to talk about when it is your talk that stops me from doing my job. We have ten minutes to work out something. If we cannot, we must try again tomorrow at 1:20. Tell me what I can do to help you be quiet. I will listen to your solution.

This conversation can continue. The age of the pupil does not matter. If the teacher treats the problem as a shared adult one, then 99% of pupils will co-operate especially once the child realizes that teacher is serious and not going to give up. The teacher is *asking* for what s/he wants, instead of demanding compliance in the traditional way. Of course, it is time-intensive and you cannot do it with every pupil. This type of process is reserved for the persistent offender who might respond by building a relationship with the teacher. It will work if the pupil is *able* to be quiet while teacher is talking to a group. He *can* already sit in assembly?

Billie	I haven't a solution, miss.
Jasmin	I have thought of four that might work, Billie, and I'll let you choose.
	1. I will sit you to one side away from everyone.
	2. You can sit by me all the time and I will touch you if you forget.
	3. We will meet every day at 1:20 when you forget.
	4. Every day you do it well I will give you a reward that we agree on.
	You can choose and if this does not work, I will have next choice. OK?

The request will work when the pupil discovers what is in compliance for him or her and realizes that the teacher means it. The request will work because people like to please. If the pupil can see that s/he is pleasing the teacher, then please the teacher they invariably will, at least until secondary school. Then peer and game-playing norms may interfere. Even then, private dialogues can be very successful. The only way to get an adolescent onside is to challenge them in private or in negotiation with a senior and allow them to save face. However, these kinds of strategies go by the wayside when dealing with trivialities. These strategies are time-intensive and emotionally demanding, and are to be used when there are *serious* educational issues to consider.

Traditional-style teaching says pupils and students are to be seen and not heard; theirs is to be taught and to absorb. Parents, the public, systems, all believe it is easy to tell the young to shut up, and they do. They try telling them to shut up at home and get rebellion. They think teachers have a secret formula: 'Teacher should be able to get on with teaching because children are socialized to quiet behaviour while teacher teaches....' It doesn't really work that way.

In the real world, human relationships must be established before the task can be accomplished. But in the real world, when a manager shouts at clients they go away. Children do the same, perhaps not in body, but definitely in mind. Schooling is becoming more like the *real* world, with parents shopping for schools and schools wooing clients. Teachers, in the new real world, cannot rely on traditional position power. Most of the time, teachers telling pupils and students to shut up does not work. Each teacher, supported by a school team, must acquire personal power.

When teachers have personal power they can give it to the system. Assertiveness gives a teacher a personal power base that works with everyone in the system from pupils to director. It is not a technique for *winning*. It is a set of principles for behaving professionally. Learning to ask for what you want is a prime skill in gaining the personal power that will make education work. To claim that personal power the teacher must know what s/he wants and how to ask for it in a way that keeps people onside. The rule is that you can ask for anything you want. You can do this because everyone has the right to refuse. You must put your energy into the request and resource it with time and effort. Jasmin will now do it with another of her wants.

Jasmin implements an I message – Going to a Seminar

Jasmin has a lot of pupils with statemented needs. She is becoming exhausted as she uses every strategy she knows to get children onside and use assertive interactions instead of aggressive ordering. Most of the pupils are used to aggressive/submissive worlds. She knows that assertiveness is the management style she wants to use, but realizes that special pupils need extra strategies. She has discovered a seminar coming up in November and she wants to go. Again, she maps out the steps towards achieving her goal:

What is wanted?	To go to a seminar on managing conflict.
Who to ask?	The Head.
Who can say yes?	Unsure. The Head, governors, advisory teacher.
What is Head's view?	Good idea, no money;
	not necessary;
	poor seminar, not recommended.
How to ask?	In private;
	state problem, identify solutions,
	give preferred solution.
Plan and rehearse:	Either role-play to reduce anxiety, or visualize possible scenes with preferred solution.

After planning and rehearsal, she approaches the Head.

Jasmin   Head, could I speak with you for ten minutes now or is there a better time later today? [The time period is controlled, with some choice for Head.]

Head	Now is fine, Jasmin, if it will only take ten minutes.
Jasmin	I *feel* I need some help in handling my class. [Using honesty and openness.] I have thought about solutions quite a bit and I think the Conflict Management Seminar in November will give me some new skills for working with my statemented children. Would you be able to release me for the day?
Head	Not easy. We overspent our budget on behaviour management last year, and I do not think the governors would approve a request from me for you to attend. Can we think of another way to get you some additional skills?
Jasmin	I have thought about it for three weeks and can only see the seminar.
Head	Leave it with me, Jasmin, and I will think about it.
Jasmin	How soon can I check with you? [Time control is still important.]
Head	On Friday, after I have spoken with the chair of governors.
Jasmin	Enrolments close on that day. Can I check with you by 1 p.m. so that I ring if funds are found?
Head	Yes.

The assertive Head has to evaluate the request alongside other priorities. Jasmin knows this, but Jasmin has the right to ask, the right to not assume a NO. Even if the answer is no, Jasmin will know that she did her best. She gave an *I* message and related it to the needs of the school. She had anticipated a no-funds response and was prepared in her planning for a special request to go to the chair of governors, hence her persistence in getting a solution before the deadline. She is not a victim of her beliefs or anxieties, but instead has exercised competence by using her assertive skills.

If this seminar is very important to her she might decide to go into more moves in the negotiation. She could suggest that funds from another source be found, for example, her personal training budget, or from her Personal Review preparation, if the school has arrived at this stage of its corporate development. Perhaps money could come from the contingency fund. The experienced, assertive teacher accompanies her request with a solution or a series of them (as Jasmin did with Billie), so that the task of the Head is easier.

Jasmin shared her problem with the Head; it is now an issue to be solved. The Head's solution may not be Jasmin's solution. It may be different. The Head may return with a yes. Jasmin is giving the Head an opportunity to serve her and be pleasing. People like to please others. Whatever the solution, Jasmin must not forget the thank you. The process is as important as the solution. Having this process for asking gives personal power to the asker, no matter what the outcome of the request. And so Jasmin continues down her list . . .

Jasmin requests repair work

The classroom needs a lot of repair work. Every room does. Instead of making a long list and doing the dramatic act, Jasmin decides she will make a priority list and, while putting it in to the deputy as per the system, she will act on one point per week:

What is wanted?	A new lock on the door.
Who to ask?	The premises officer/deputy.
Who can mend it?	The premises officer.
What is officer's view?	Too much to do. Do it officially as per lists.
How to ask?	Visit officer's premises, state problem, give solution.
Plan and rehearse:	Role-play or visualize (knowing officer).

Jasmin's approach to the premises office could be responded to in a few ways:

Jasmin	Oh, Mr Stan, I have a number of room problems and I have made my list. Would you glance at it with me and tell me how long it might take?
Officer	If you teachers looked after ... *or*
	Yes, of course. But I can do nothing till ... *or*
	Let's have a look ... oh, I'll do that today and ... .

Jasmin has asked properly. She has not tried to manipulate the officer with either submissive approaches, such as 'Oh, please, please help me. I cannot cope ... I'll do *anything*!' or aggressive approaches, 'Keeper, if you don't, I'll ....'

Premises officers have many requests a day, most of them repetitive and most of them arising because of human error. If this is Jasmin's error, a request which reveals human vulnerability with dignity is appropriate. This means Jasmin can ask without putting herself down. It *does* mean she can say, 'I have broken the lock again and I feel an idiot every time I look at it because it reminds me of my stupidity. Could you mend it again, please?'

Assertiveness is not an android's language. It is a language which reveals feelings and failings. It is the language used by someone with high self-esteem and it can be used to lift self-esteem. It is open, honest and without a hidden agenda. Jasmin's self-esteem is OK whether she gets what she asks for or not, because she knows that she has asked in the right way and she is acting with integrity.

The possibility of her getting what she wants is increased when she:

has a clear vision of what she wants
uses a personal *I*
builds in choices for the giver
plans and rehearses so that she is ready to negotiate.

Jasmin accommodates a No response – No Friday duty

Jasmin	(To assembled staff) I have a request to make, that I hope someone can help me with. Doing playground duty on a Friday is stressing me out. [She is being honest, with no false, professional pride.] Will anyone swap with me?
Mary	No way, Friday's a lousy day.
Prendip	I have music straight after play, sorry.
Bill	I'll think about it.
Roshea	Come back to me if no one volunteers.
Jeannie	That's not a fair request. I had to do it all last year, and I didn't ask.
Vicha	I suppose you want me to do it. I get stuck with all the nasties.

Jasmin has asked and, in asking, has increased her chances of getting what she wants by 95%. She can take advantage of Vicha's self-sabotage or accept Roshea's offer. The risk she took was getting some abuse, from Jeannie, and some rejection, from Mary and Prendip, but she got some co-operation from Bill and Roshea.

Asking means being more vulnerable. You may have to reveal some things about yourself that you prefer to keep hidden. Revealing weakness is not to be taken lightly, as some people do take advantage of the vulnerability of others. However, asking for asking's sake is not an assertive behaviour. The asking must come from a genuine need. If asking results in many 'no' responses, then the asker must examine his or her goals and the process that is being used.

Many teachers are put off asking because they fear a 'no' response. It is because the other has the right to say no that the request is permissible in the first place. An assertive request leaves room for the other to say no. You have that right and in exercising it you must take the consequences. You have the right to ask for anything you want because other people have the right to say no. In respecting others' right to say no, there is no manipulation when you ask for something.

A submissive person would probably preface their request with 'You'll probably say no, but I'll ask anyway' or 'I'm desperate or I wouldn't ask . . . .' An aggressive one would probably begin with 'You owe me one' or 'Don't dare say no because . . . .' Both anticipate a 'no' because they know their motive is unjust or they believe they do not have the right to ask.

Some people can *sound* assertive and *be* manipulative: the proof is in how the giver feels afterwards. If bad feeling results for the giver, then the transaction was not an open one. If you use assertive techniques just to get your own way, you will get a reputation for exacting favours!

Jasmin was assertive. She had her list of wants which she decided she could ask for and asked for what she felt was reasonable. Some may think that she asked for too much and that others would be deprived if Jasmin got what she wanted. Asking is not the result, only the beginning. Everyone has the right to ask and everyone has the right to say no. Some very persuasive teachers appear to get more than their due. The assertive teacher is realistic, asks for what is honestly wanted in the best way possible and allows the other the privilege of saying yes or no.

Exercises

1. Complete each of the following with a *real* request:

    I would be pleased if you would ...
    Will you help me to ...
    I need someone to ...
    May I ...
    I want ...

2. Change these by removing the reason/excuse/excessive politeness:

    My little girl is allergic to smoke. Would you ...
    My head hurts, please, please will ...
    You can see me struggling with this load ...
    If you don't mind, I have a sore back and I ...
    I hate to disturb you, forgive me, but, would you be so very kind and ...

3. List five things you would like to ask others to do for you.

    Why would you say no to each?
    Why would you say yes to each?
    Why would they say yes/no to you?

Actions to take

Notice your feelings prior to, during, and after asking the following. Remember to be direct. Their actual response does not matter. The focus here is on how you feel when they say no, yes or stall. Feelings are explored later.

> Ask a fellow teacher to speak to a parent for you about a certain child.
> Ask a senior staff member to give your shoulders a quick massage.
> Ask a parent to send some magazines to school.
> Ask a pupil to carry a heavy load for you.
> Ask the Head if you can leave ten minutes early.
> Ask a colleague to go to the theatre with you in the near future.

4 Saying No and setting limits

In brief

- **Saying No is a choice assertive people exercise.**
  Deciding when to say No, is the testing part for teachers.
- **Say No to the request and Yes to the person.**
  Once No is the decision, the assertive teachers can say it without offence.
- **A No delivered assertively is quite acceptable.**
  No indicates that a teacher has set some boundaries on how to deploy their time, energy and expertise.
- **A No can be constructive.**
  A No in the right place improves teacher performance and satisfaction.
- **Setting limits is an option.**
  When teachers choose not to say No they can still set limits.
- **A No can be overruled.**
  Teachers can accommodate No overrulings.

'No' is a choice

Teachers have a lot of demands on their time, energy and expertise. If they do not say No to inappropriate requests, they will be unable to give their best to the things that matter. The effects of not saying no vary from minor stress to burnout or illness, from a job just done to a job done so badly that it were better it were not done at all. The effects of not saying No are felt not only by the individual but by the pupils and the school itself as well.

Teachers often have a problem saying No. There are many reasons for this. These include not wanting to say No, seeing no good reason to say No, respecting authority, fearing repercussions, or just believing they should say Yes. In professions where there are needy people, it is all too easy for professionals to extend themselves to meet the needs of others. The element of *vocation* drives many teachers to serve at the expense of themselves. In the short term, that may be fine; in the long term, it creates inefficiency and burnout.

Saying No is only an option when the teacher wants to say it. A good indicator of whether a No should have been said is the feeling that accompanies the carrying-out of the request. If the teacher feels bad then s/he should have said No.

Deciding to say No

There are some very good reasons for not saying No and there are some very good reasons for saying No. Identifying when to say No is the difficult part.

The following case studies demonstrate some of the dilemmas associated with saying No.

Case Study: Roger, 29, secondary English teacher

Roger lives for school. He teaches a maximum load, works with underachieving volunteers in the lunch time, runs a magazine club after school and he takes private students in the evenings. He runs the staff social calendar, collects for three charities and is teacher representative on the board of governors. He says Yes to every request made of him, whether he can do it well or not. He does some things well; others, satisfactorily, and yet others poorly, but he does not say No.

Roger appears to not know that the word No exists. If he does, he does not know he has a right to use it or does not exercise his right to use it. He is not a problem to himself in the short term. However, he may be a problem to the staff if he is holding so many areas of responsibility and not doing them well, or if he is preventing others from contributing. Though he is performing the tasks and achieving some of his goals, his relationships are poor. Some colleagues even resent his eagerness because it puts them in a poor light. Becoming assertive is not an issue for Roger but others around him may have to be assertive if they wish to assume some of his roles.

It would probably take a crisis of some kind for Roger to become self-aware. Then he might reflect on his situation and see the lack of balance in his life. Education may have benefited, and probably still does, from the dedication of the Rogers to their tasks.

Case Study: Kashi, 58, Head of History Department

Kashi wants to say No to the many requests he receives to speak at conferences and seminars. He has been doing it for over 20 years and he is tired. He just wants to let all that go. However, as the representative of an eastern European culture which no longer exists, he feels it is his duty to pass on his understanding of a life now gone.

He carries on with his speaking engagements until he develops palpitations and dizzy spells every time he has to speak. He pulls out at the last minute three times and finally they stop asking him. His reputation suffers at the end because he has let people down. Kashi submissively gave in to the requests until ill health said No for him.

An assertive Kashi would have listened to his own inner voice and feelings, thanked the organizers for their invitations, and declined. He needed to re-appraise his sense of duty. If he felt his message was needed he could have set limits. To continue disseminating his message he could have pursued other options, for example, writing or recording his memoirs.

Case Study: Preyma, 33, Deputy Head, junior school

Preyma feels very much under the microscope as she comes to the end of her first year as a deputy in a inner-city primary school. She takes her role in staff development very seriously. Her empathy and excellent listening skills draw to her all those with problems. Every lunch time and after school there is someone with her, pouring out their problems. She is feeling the strain. The role of counsellor is now dominating her time and her attention to other areas of responsibility are being neglected. The Head had spoken to her about this. She has a dilemma. She feels that if she says No to the people who need her support, they will feel let down. If she says No to the Head's request to redirect her time and energy, she will earn the disapproval of the Head. And both will think she wasn't up to the job.

Preyma must start by deciding what she wants as her professional goal, then develop her strategic and tactical plan and negotiate with the Head. Then she must say No to things which are outside her purpose, or at least set limits on how much of her time, energy and expertise are to go that way.

Saying No, after she has said Yes for almost a year, will be quite hard for her. An assertive Preyma would act before the need to say No arose. She would disclose her need for more time in the new school year to devote to other areas of her responsibility. She would ask those who needed the kind of support she had been giving to make other arrangements. This may mean she is assertively helpful, finding the names of some counsellors she would recommend or at least a contact point for each.

In schools this kind of support is traditionally very personal and casual. If the school as an autonomous workplace assumes personnel functions similar to public and private bodies, then the human resource function will include the *care* role for someone with designated resources. This is not the case for Preyma. If she respects herself and her career she will take advantage of the Head's feedback and the time of year to make this change.

Case Study: Colleen, 27, primary teacher

Colleen works with Cindy. They are friends both in and out of school. They share a common class space and their children intermingle. Cindy is going through a bad patch with her boyfriend and is having a lot of time off school. Quite often Colleen has to manage the two classes with the aid of two classroom assistants, at least until a supply arrives. This means that Colleen is really doing double work.

Cindy rang one Sunday evening and told Colleen that she would not be in for the next two days as she and her boyfriend had just made up and were going to Paris that night to get married. She asked Colleen to tell the Head she was ill and to cover for her. Colleen was horrified. She knew the supply budget was spent, that Cindy was unreliable and likely to take the whole week, and that she would have to lie to the Head. She wanted to say No. An assertive Colleen would simply say, 'No, Cindy, I am your friend and colleague and I am upset and disappointed that you would ask me to tell that lie. I will not do that for you as perjuring myself will damage both me and my career, and our friendship.'

Once you know you want to say No, you still have to work out HOW to do it appropriately.

Say No to the request and Yes to the person

The Head may have to ask Roger to not say Yes. Kashi could have said No to speaking and Yes to sending some material. Preyma can say No and help staff find alternative care. It is possible to say No and keep the relationship. Colleen must manage this delicate task. Assertive language will let her do that.

How to say No

The No should be definite; there should be no tones of doubt, defence, or revenge. The No should define the relationship and use the name of the requester, for example, 'Roger, I am saying No to your offer of representing the staff. Thank you for your co-operation in volunteering.' The No should be accompanied by a description of how the giver feels about saying No: 'I feel very sad to have to say No to your invitation. I do enjoy speaking about life in the twenties. I hope you find someone else easily.'

The assertive No does not need a reason attached. Listening to men and women saying No is very interesting. Men do not smile when they give a No, women often do. Men rarely give a reason for a No. Women almost always give a reason. Men's No is generally accepted at face value, women's is usually the start of a persuasion campaign. The staffroom is no different from the rest of the world.

Imagine this scene, typically set in a school office with four teachers present. The secretary has a parent on the telephone and needs assistance. Note who does not use the word No at all!

Secretary	Who will speak with this parent about Sports' Day?
Bob	No, not me.
Col	Sorry, no.
Mary	I am rather busy and they ask so many questions I cannot answer.
Connie	I'd rather somebody else did it; I messed up the details last time.

The No does not need a reason. However, sometimes it is political or tactful to do so. It is interesting that women are more political and tactful than men, and to their cost! If a reason is deemed to be necessary, the No should be accompanied by a reason which shows the tangible effects of complying with the request.

Bob	Not me, I must have this with the Head in three minutes.
Col	Sorry, no. I am not involved in the Sports' Day.
Mary	No, I do not have any of the details and would only confuse them.
Connie	No, the best person to speak with them is Mr X.

Too often the reason is an excuse which allows the other to argue round it and dismiss the reasons. Mary would be the person most likely to end up speaking, because her No is the weakest. The No can be accompanied by an alternative offer which the refuser wants to make. This often is the way to make it clear that you are refusing the request not the person.

Connie	No, I will not speak to them, but I will get the programme from next door for you to read bits to them.

The assertive No is genuinely given and received

Case Study: Helena, 36, primary teacher

Helena worked very hard and insisted on excellence from herself in all aspects of her professional life. Her room was immaculate, her displays magnificent and her children's bookwork the pride of the school. She had returned to teaching two years earlier and she kept herself to herself. No one knew anything of her personal life or previous experience. The chair of governors was very impressed with her presentation work and asked the Head to persuade her to accept responsibility for the school's centenary open day exhibition of work, in four months' time.

The Head broached the topic of the centenary exhibition in staff meeting and called for volunteers to accept responsibility for sections of the activities. She then asked Helena directly to take charge of the visual displays, explaining how the chair of governors had herself suggested Helena take charge.

Helena did not like to say No. She had been asked in front of everyone and all had said how well she would do it. But she was tired. She felt drained. She did not feel she could accept one more bit of responsibility because her family situation was already testing her too far and she was only just managing the school part of her life. To accept more would be too much.

In the staff meeting she avoided any commitment, just smiled and listened to the comments. She could say Yes and stagger through, or say Yes and then withdraw on some excuse. She wanted to say No. How could she say No? She played the scene in her mind that night.

Helena	Head, could I have a word about the Centenary?
Head	Yes, Helena. We are so lucky to have you at this time. Your skill in this area is a real bonus.
Helena	Well, I don't want to do it. Don't ask me. It wasn't fair the way you asked. You called for volunteers for everything else and then named me deliberately. You gave me no real choice in front of the whole staff. It really was most unfair. You don't know what I have to put up with at home and I only just cope at school. You just assume too much.

That's what she would break down and say! Her feelings would rule her and she would really throw herself into trouble. This response would be aggressive. It is blaming, full of accusative *yous*. It will damage the relationship between the two of them. It would take an extraordinary Head to manage this. Or Helena might make her needs known indirectly:

| Helena | I'm not going to do it. She had no right to put me on the spot like that. I think it is most unfair. She didn't ask anyone else directly. |
| Colleague | That's right. |

Some time later, Helena's colleague would relay Helena's feelings to the Head. Letting the message get to the Head by an indirect route avoids the confrontation. However, the relationship would be damaged and the matter would still not be settled, because the Head would be sure to want to know why, so confrontation would still occur. She explored more direct responses:

| Helena | Head, about the Centenary, I must decline your kind invitation. Thank you for asking but the answer is No. |

Dare she? Dare she deliver a No with no reason, straight, definite No, body language and words completely congruent? However, Helena's relationship with the Head is important and this response shows no respect for their relationship, or anyone's right to ask for what they want. She tries a direct, but less aggressive, tactic:

Helena	Head, I cannot do the Centenary display because I already have too much to do.
Head	Oh, Helena, we will give you some time off class to do it. We would not expect you to do it all in your own time.
Helena	Oh, but I think my class is more important, Head. I do not want to neglect my work with them.
Head	That's OK, Helena. You can set the work and I will get a supply to cover. They will not suffer.
Helena	But Head, I do not like anyone else taking my class.
Head	Helena. You have the best talent for this job. This display is the best PR for the school. I want to deploy your talents this way. Your class will be covered.

Here, Helena has presented a case and been overruled. In giving reasons she has provided an opportunity for the Head to counter all her excuses and then use position power to get what she wants. The relationship is damaged when power divides them. Helena responds:

| Helena | I understand that I am the best person for the display work, Head. I have a problem, however. If I accept this responsibility I will be stressed beyond my acceptable levels and all my work will suffer. At the moment I am only just balancing my responsibilities. Please do not ask me to accept this extra responsibility right now. |

What can a Head say to this? Helena has made herself vulnerable here, in revealing her real reason for not wanting to accept the responsibility. She has protected herself with restricting her problem to *right now*. The relationship is not damaged. The Head has a problem. It is less of a problem than if Helena goes off sick. Helena can help the Head to solve this problem. If she does this, she will be volunteering some help in reaching a solution. She can say:

Helena   Head, I have a suggestion. I will create a design that someone else can follow and I will monitor the progress of student work under the direction of someone else who is responsible for the whole display.

A No can be constructive

By offering suggestions and alternatives, Helena is behaving professionally. In saying No she is conserving her time, energy and expertise at a time when she knows that to do otherwise would interfere with her primary purpose which is the education of her group of children. She is not saying No on a whim, or just to save herself work. In making an offer after her No has been accepted, she is, in effect, setting limits rather than refusing a request. If she had offered as part of the refusal she would have been bargaining or negotiating.

Saying No is an option. The repercussions of a No can be managed. The way to do this will be determined by the importance of the relationship. In schools, relationships are important and need to be protected. Assertiveness confers professionalism on interactions by demonstrating both self-respect and respect for the other. Not saying No for fear of rejection, disapproval, contempt, revenge, guilt or punishment undermines self-esteem. Not saying No because of an unexamined inherited belief in tradition, cultural expectation or conformity to 'shoulds' is blindness. Professionals cannot afford either low self-esteem or blindness.

The practicalities of saying No

The body language for a No involves a straight spine, the head straight, and the arms relaxed at the sides. The person saying No should maintain eye contact but should not smile. The inner dialogues must be on the refuser's side and deal with the feelings, particularly any guilt.

Of course, if the teacher is manipulatively saying No, just testing to see how a No goes, then this will show. What makes the No work is the sincerity of the refuser. This genuineness is hard to achieve if the inner voice is saying 'I really should say yes.' A good way to deal with this is to say assertively, 'I feel guilty saying No, yet I really do not want to do this, so I am saying No and accepting the guilt.' Honesty makes the refuser vulnerable.

The decision-making process

Ask yourself if you want to say Yes or No. *Feel* your answer as well as hear it. If both head and heart agree, just do it. If you are at war with yourself then check your motives for a Yes and for a No, and determine where your integrity is. List the possible repercussions of No and consider if you can live with them. Choose to say No in a manner that will help the relationship.

If you are only saying No to make a point, then admit it: 'I will say No because I want to stress ... .' If you decide to set limits instead of saying No, put yourself in the shoes of the other who will hear your message and decide if the relationship would be damaged and if that matters.

Saying No

Strengthen it with:	Definitely not.
Reinforce it with:	I do not want to do that.
Expand it with:	No, I feel that would not suit me.
Reveal feelings:	No, I feel upset that you have asked me.
Illuminate further:	No, I feel angry that you believe I would do that because I do not do those kinds of things.
Give a single reason:	No, I cannot do that because I will be away.
Use the broken record:	I will be away, I will be away. No, I will be away.

These words can be said in a hundred different ways. It is important to say them and mean them. A half-hearted No will be interpreted as a partial Yes or *persuade me*! Avoid sarcastic expressions like 'What part of NO don't you understand?' or 'No is a two-letter word', or 'No is not a four-letter word.' Do not assume that a Yes or No has to be given immediately. Assertive teachers can ask for time to consider and specify when they will know:

Allie   I do not want to answer Yes or No now. I will think about it and
             give you an answer at 7 p.m. When must you know by?

When a No is met with 'You have always said Yes before', the assertive
teacher can agree: 'You are right, in the past I have said Yes.' In adding more
Noes to their vocabulary, teachers should be aware that they will be
challenged until they have demonstrated that they are genuine about it.

The no No option or when a No is refused

Teachers know that there are times when a No response is not expedient, no
matter how much they want to use it. It may be a principle, a value position
that is dear to the teacher, and it may create a dilemma. If the teacher gives
in with a 'What's the use?' capitulation or mounts a high horse with a 'That's
the last straw,' then the teacher loses. The teacher must try for a no-lose
outcome.

The Stockholm option – which gained its name when terrorists (Baader-
Meinhoff) held hostages in Stockholm in the early 1970s – is a relation of
Hobson's choice. It provides no choice because the other has total power and
can override any No; Hobson's choice is a choice of one. A No in this context
is a waste of time.

The assertive teacher has to say Yes. The teacher can choose to override a
personal principle on a particular occasion without a loss of self-esteem. The
ideal self often has to check with reality. This need not be a drop in personal
standards. The assertive teacher can be pragmatic because the world is not
ideal. A positive inner voice allows the teacher to give the self permission to
step outside the usual principle and the message delivered can be 'I want to
say No. I want you to know that I am going against my principles on this
when I do not say No.'

Generally, however, the matter is not so serious. If there is a genuine
ideal that must be adhered to, then the professional can take the risk and
stick with the No:

Teacher 1   It will cost me to say No. I have a firm policy of never giving
             money to charity, and I must stand outside the staff decision on
             this occasion.
Teacher 2   It would be expedient to say Yes. However, if I did I would be
             breaking one of my most dearly held principles. I believe ... .

When a teacher decides to override a personal ideal, s/he can say:

Teacher 3   Generally I would say No to doing detention duty because I do not believe that detentions are helpful in promoting new behaviours for children. I will do it because on this occasion I respect your need for help.

Teacher 4 I want to say No as my past experience of saying Yes has not been good; I am willing to say Yes on this occasion, and see how I feel.

When a teacher has an inner conflict, when thoughts say one thing and feelings say another, there is another kind of dilemma. Which should be heard? Which should be listened to? Some listen to their thoughts, some to their feelings. Taking a risk and reflecting on the results is the only answer. No matter how firmly a No is delivered it is sometimes unacceptable.

Head I am sorry, I cannot accept a No. You will take Jeremy back into your class.

Position power can override assertiveness. The assertive teacher does not always *win*. Assertiveness is not about winning. Assertiveness is about playing the game with integrity. Position power can override assertiveness, but it cannot take away a teacher's dignity. Too many teachers give away power by bestowing power on authority. Assertiveness, by focusing on rights and responsibilities, gives teachers a sense of their place in the scheme of things. This in turn gives them personal power.

Exercises

1. List five requests made of you that you would like to say No to.
   What stops you?
   Is there a common reason? For example, do they all contain a 'should'?

2. Plan to say No next time the request is made. Choose one of the options below. Which No will you choose? Why?
   A straight No.
   A No with a reason.
   A No and share your feeling for doing so.
   A No and offer an alternative.
   A mixture of the above.

3. Visualize the scene and see your No being accepted. Get someone to role-play the scene with you. You be the requester, while the other tries the Noes, then change. Discuss your feelings about it.

Action to take

Find a real-life situation and say No. Manage the repercussions.

5 Assertive helping styles

In brief

- **Helping others with problems is a choice.**
  Teachers choose to be helpers, both in their professional and personal lives.
- **Effective helping is skill-based if the helped is to benefit long-term.**
  Assertive helping effectively meets the need of the other because it enables the helped to develop skills.
- **Unskilled helpers often block the helper.**
  Teachers who combine skills with genuine motives for helping are valuable professionals in a people-based industry.
- **Intervention needs special mediation skills.**
  Teachers often have to intervene to stop problems spreading and to protect their own relationship with the protagonists.
- **Helping has some dangers attached.**
  When teachers are tempted to adopt counselling as a prime role, their teaching suffers.

Helping is a choice

Teachers are helpers, advisers, counsellors and enablers; it is easy for them to put their own needs to one side and help others. Helping is putting one's own agenda to one side and clearing a space so that one can focus on the other person's issues. This involves putting one's own 'shoulds' and other judgements and resulting advice away.

The role of helper involves, first of all, listening. It involves working with the other to identify the real problem and generate solutions. The helper supports the evaluation of options, choosing one while maintaining a selection of back-up options. Together, the helper and helped plan a strategy or tactic, with the helper providing necessary support and offering advice when it is deliberately requested.

In order for help to be accepted, there must be a relationship. Strangers can and do provide help, and the very nature of the objective relationship can be useful when anonymity is in some way needed. The teaching role, however, demands that there be a relationship of respect between the helper and the helped.

When an assertive teacher sees a problem s/he decides whose problem it is. If s/he decides it is his/her problem, then s/he uses confrontation skills. If s/he decides the other has the problem then the helping skills become important.

Helpers need skills which enable the other to problem-solve

Non-assertive helpers rush in with responses which either deny a problem or its importance, or take the spotlight and claim a similar problem. Common responses include: 'If I were you' (over-riding), 'Let me do it for you' (rescuing), or 'Oh, that happened to me' (thunder-stealing). None of these responses respect the right of the other to have a problem or find their own solution. Non-assertive helpers use gate-slammers that effectively close down dialogue. For example:

- No more, off you go. Don't talk like that. I want you to forget it.
- If you do that, you will regret it. I know because ... .
- Well, you shouldn't act like that. You should be more friendly.
- Why don't you go and try again? This time I'm sure he'll say Yes.
- The only logical thing to do is to stand your ground and practise some more.
- You are just too lazy to do it. Pull your finger out and get it done.
- You're a typical quitter, just like a woman when things get tough.
- Because you did that, this will now happen and then he will be upset again.
- You can cope, you always do. You always come out on top.

Intentions may be good, but dismissing the problem or its importance to the other is not being helpful. It just makes the person with a problem feel they are not understood.

Assertive helping involves time and energy

The first rule of the assertive helper is to resource the situation with time and attention. If the problem has high feeling evident, the need for help might be urgent. The assertive helper must decide if they can give time and energy right then.

Case Study: Mavis, 49, secondary teacher

Mavis was rushing to go home when she saw Maria, the Head, obviously upset. She wondered if she should stop and see what the matter was. She had ten minutes before she absolutely had to leave so she decided to follow her into the office.

Maria	Oh, Mavis, thank goodness it's you and not anyone else.
Mavis	Is something wrong?
Maria	Oh, that dreadful man. He threatened me and said I had not heard the last of it. He is going to the Director.
Mavis	I don't understand, Maria, but I can hear you are very upset and worried.
Maria	Yes, I am upset, but no, I am not worried. Frustrated at the thought of all the time this is going to take. If I don't tell someone, I'll burst.
Mavis	I know it helps to tell someone. I have ten minutes before I must leave, will that help? I cannot stay longer but you could give me an outline and ring me after seven.
Maria	Well, two months ago … .

Ten minutes later, Mavis is still listening and she knows she has not *helped* yet. Maria is unaware of the time.

Mavis	I am sorry to interrupt, Maria, because I must leave. I want to help. I may be able to help you sort out the main points. Would you like to ring me at 7 p.m. and we will go through it?

What Mavis has done is help to the limit of her current resources. She knows if she stays now she will start to resent the fact that she is there because she should be helping somewhere else. She would then not be focusing on Maria's problem but her own. She had set a limit on the time and she had to keep it. Offering to help later was a door-opener that invited Maria to continue, if she felt the need.

Non-assertive teachers might feel guilty at limiting help in this way. Perhaps once in a while it may be necessary to go beyond the set limits. If, however, it is a pattern that the helper always overruns the limit, then there is a need to become assertive. When the help is taking the helper from something important, then the help being given is probably not as good as it could be when resourced sufficiently. When the helping is persistently done at the expense of the helper, resentment builds eventually and breaks the relationship.

Helping assertively means engaging with the other's feelings

The second rule of the assertive helper is to respond to the feeling in the voice of the person who needs help. The feeling can govern the response – a smile, a hug, a simple 'I feel for you', an expression of commiseration. Identifying the feeling is not easy and requires more than passive or reflective listening. It needs *active* listening. Active listening is more than understanding meaning; it is recognizing and empathizing with the speaker's feeling.

Case Study: Steve, 33, special support teacher, primary

Steve spends a lot of his time working with the travellers' children. He often finds he has to counsel teachers, including Neville, who are driven to despair by the interrupted progress of their students. A non-assertive helper responds to Neville's complaint:

Neville	I don't know, I just feel I am wasting my time with Billie.
Carl	Oh, you shouldn't feel like that. That's stupid. I felt like that once and now ... .
Neville	But I do feel that way and I ... oh, what the hell! Forget it!

Steve uses assertive language in this situation:

Neville	I don't know. I just think I'm getting somewhere with Billie and then he disappears again. Carl says I am stupid for feeling like this.
Steve	I sense you are feeling frustrated at not being able to help Billie more. That is understandable. As for being stupid, far from it. Billie uses the school system and combines it with a family culture which is different from ours.
Neville	But I think he would rather be at school and I get angry at his

Steve   parents for denying him the educational advantages of his peers.
            I understand that anger. I feel it sometimes, too.

Steve does not have to make sense of Neville or psychologically analyse him. He just has to show he understands and empathizes. Too often teachers take the responsibility of sorting out other people's irrationalities with logical responses to worries. Until a person asks for direction it is preferable to withhold comment and advice.

Assertive helping language can sound very phoney at first. The standard '... and how do you feel about this?' is almost a joke. Assertive scripting certainly is phoney. It is phoney because the learner is using somebody else's language at first. So it is not genuine. The learner is consciously learning new dialogue. Once it is internalized the learner can speak genuinely, with personal dialogue.

Carl Rogers, the US psychologist, once said that it was the attitude of the helper that was more important than any skill or training. This is true when the helper is assertive. The motive of an assertive helper is to respond to the feelings of the person with a problem and help them arrive at a reasonable way of dealing with any issue or problem.

Assertive helpers know why *they are being helpful*

The third rule of assertive helping is to know your motive. The best motive is a genuine desire to be helpful. In some ways it is easier to help another sort out a problem than sort out one of one's own. There is power in helping others, but there is more power in helping the self. The assertive helper helps others but not at the expense of the self, nor in return for favours or for exacting favours.

The assertive teacher is not a professional helper. Many skills and much training are involved in that. The assertive helper knows how to be a friend when someone needs one. That friend volunteers when distress or a problem becomes evident. That help has three characteristics: a genuine desire to help, a willingness to put aside one's own agenda, and an understanding of the feelings of the person in need.

The assertive teacher as interventionist

Sometimes there is a problem between two or more others and the assertive outsider can help. Intervening is not easy. The police know to their peril how intervention in domestic violence cases backfires. Teachers can learn from that, particularly when intervening in children's or friends' interpersonal problems.

Sometimes intervention is necessary from a professional point of view or desirable from a personal or professional point of view. Sometimes, intervention is requested. No matter why intervention occurs, the assertive teacher can contribute positively providing impartiality is accompanied by the openness and honesty that respects integrity.

Case Study: Alistair, 30, primary teacher

There were many fights and arguments in the playground and Alistair had no choice but to intervene as part of his job. He could submissively avoid it, pretend not to see many of the interactions and hope they would blow over. He could aggressively march over and without any attempt at investigation, *sort it out*. What teacher hasn't, and what teacher won't continue to do so at times in the future? Assertion is about situational choice from a position of personal power.

This day Alistair saw Kwesi and Brian, at each other's throats yet again. He physically pulled them apart. Kwesi was particularly upset and was blabbering on about Brian calling him names, tripping him up and kicking him when he was playing British bulldog He said he did nothing to cause this. In fact he said he tried to get away, but Brian came after him. Brian said nothing. Kwesi said Brian was always following him after school and if he told anyone Brian and his big brother would beat him up. All this without Alistair having to say a word.

The assertive Alistair, avoiding verbalizing his prejudged assumption that Brian was bullying yet another peer, acted on feelings first.

Alistair	Kwesi, you are very upset, take four deep breaths. Brian, you are very tense, breathe deeply. All the rest of you move away, if I need any of you I will call you.
Boy	I saw it, sir. I know what happened … sir, it happened to me … .
Alistair	Enough, move away.
Alistair	Now I am taking you both inside and we are going to talk about what has happened. You can have three sentences each and then I will ask you both some questions. Then we will decide together what should happen next.

Kwesi repeated the story of being picked on. Brian was silent until Alistair said he would have to accept Kwesi's version of events and report a case of unfair harassment to the Head. He asked Brian if that was what should happen next. Still silence. He asked Kwesi what he wanted to happen next. Kwesi said he wanted Brian to stop picking on him and stop following him after school. Alistair said he would tell the Head what Kwesi wanted.

In the absence of co-operation from Brian and the allegations of Kwesi, Alistair has no choice but to refer the incident for further investigation. He did not *collect evidence* from the children's peers. He only interacted at this stage with the protagonists. No matter what his own thoughts, at this stage he only acted to break up the situation and maintain his relationship with both.

This kind of intervention is what we are used to in the professional role. It seems hard to transfer it to the staffroom when personal feelings are involved. . . . Yet intervention as mediation is essentially a process which involves:

building trust   collecting data non-judgementally
focusing   clarifying and creating 'other shoe' vision
moving forward   agreeing rules and identifying acceptable solutions
confronting   bringing opponents together
acting   facilitating outcomes.

Case Study: Clive, 56, Head Teacher, secondary school

Clive had a problem. Two of his hardest-working staff members seem to have a feud. Keely and Gwen are professionally polite to each other at all times, yet every member of staff feels uncomfortable when in the presence of both of them. Their hostility to each other cannot be hidden. Clive has admitted that it is interfering with the harmony of the staff and that he must bring the conflict into the open. He dreads it; they are both strong women. What are his choices? He can:

- do nothing and hope it will go away of its own accord
- bring it up in staff meeting
- ask every member of staff their thoughts and invite them to say something to Keely and Gwen
- delegate the problem to his deputy
- call them into his office separately and tell each that the hostility is obvious, destructive and unacceptable, and that it must stop
- invite each to describe what the hostility is about and ask how he can help
- visit each of them in their offices and *order an end to it*, or *invite an explanation*
- call them together in his office or one of theirs and *order* or *invite*.

Choices of how to tackle this are unlimited. In real life, the benefits and costs would be clearer because the whole personalities of the people would limit the choices available. In this situation, the real life Clive summoned them to his office together and tried to make them forget previous differences, shake hands and be friends ... for his sake. It was totally inappropriate. The problem of how to mediate is his not Keely and Gwen's. Their problem is not the same as his. He should have intervened and assumed the assertive mediator role providing a structure for resolving the problem with their solutions. What Clive should have done is intervene with mediation skills.

Intervention needs mediation skills

Mediation skills include building trust, focusing the protagonists, moving the proceedings forward, confronting the issues and people, and participating in the solution selection and implementation.

- Building trust – Clive would visit each separately on their own territory and say, 'I want to draw attention to the fact that the bad feeling between you and Gwen/Keely is disturbing the staff. We have a problem and I need to be involved as it is now affecting more than just you two. Will you tell me about it?' Without judgement he would hear each account for the bad feeling. If either refused to admit the problem then a problem-solving strategy would need to accompany the assertive approach.

- Focusing the protagonists – Clive would then discuss with each the 'other shoe' vision so that each would see the repercussions of the situation continuing unresolved, perhaps saying, 'This relationship is hurting both of you and interfering with your effectiveness in the school. I want you to think about those effects and ask you to come to a meeting with me tomorrow afternoon at 2:30 p.m., so we can identify some acceptable solutions.
  Having focused on the effects, Clive would give some time for each to think and arrive at possible resolutions before going any further. Their input to the solution will ensure that it is effective and permanent.

- Moving the proceedings forward – In a second meeting, this time *on his territory,* possible solutions can be generated and he can evaluate the effects of the suggested resolutions with each person: 'I think your first and third suggestions are excellent. How do you think Gwen/Keely will respond to that? Can we do anything to make that more acceptable to G/K? Your fourth suggestion is unacceptable to me as Head.

Because it is his problem, Clive must have a say in the resolution. He must provide a framework for arriving at that solution. He will set up the meeting when he thinks there are enough suggestions for a workable solution.

● Confronting the difficulties – Soon after generating possible solutions, Clive brings Gwen and Keely together. He would draw their attention to the purpose of the meeting, that is, to resolve the difficulties they have and have been unable to resolve of their own volition. He would set up the ground rules:

> 'We have 30 minutes to arrive at a workable solution to the relationship between you that is damaging the harmony of the staff and the work environment. I have spoken with each of you and heard the suggestions you both have for resolving it. I will summarize the options I have heard from each, and ask each of you to comment in turn.'

He must take charge here because he can be devoid of feeling, and Gwen and Keely would find it difficult to do so. He does not need to be authoritarian. However, he must provide the structure for Gwen and Keely to resolve their difficulty and if they cannot, he must then become authoritarian.

● Participating in the solution – Clive must now act as referee, ensuring the rules are kept, clarifying where confusion might bog them down: 'Can I summarize? Gwen, you asked for ... and Keely, you said if ... so if we explore that we might ... We have spent seven minutes on that point and we are now going in a circle, can we discard it and move on to the next ....'

As chairman, his assertive stance will provide the structure that helps the other two to accept responsibility for the difficulty they are creating for the school as well as responsibility for resolving it. He is respecting their rights by allowing them to resolve it themselves. He can use his position power and skill assertively, instead of aggressively, because then his relationship with each will not be endangered.

It is all very well to just lay blame and say professionals should not behave like this. The reality is that they do. This situation was real: Clive had two Heads of Department at loggerheads. It went back ten years to when each had been considered for a first promotion; unfortunately the selection process had broken down and both had been told they had the position. The embarrassment, the feeling side of this, had never been dealt with and when the two found themselves on the same staff in equal positions, they brought a competitive rather than a collaborative approach to their work. This continued for eighteen more months before one of them finally left the teaching profession, burned-out because of the competitiveness.

Helping others to resolve interpersonal problems is not easy. Staffs do contain humanists and harmonizers; people who are skilled at keeping the peace. Keeping the peace means more than pushing unpleasantness away; it means confronting unpleasantness pleasantly.

The main skills of helping

Listening – Two ears, two eyes and one mouth. A ratio of four to one. The ears listen to the words and the tone, the eyes *listen* to the body language and the feelings. The mouth encourages and focuses the speaker.

Focusing – The helper helps the other to establish the real issue and generate possible choices. The helper directs with whole brain focus – 'What do you think? What do you feel?' –   Successful outcomes arise when right and left brain agree.

Motivating – The helper supports the other by using door-openers which lead the other in the direction of his or her own choice.

Evaluating – The helper provides feedback which the other can use to make a wise decision.

Advising – The helper gives advice only on the special request of the other when all resources have been exhausted.

Intervening – The helper structures a process which allows protagonists to confront their issues and arrive at win-win solutions which bring long-term resolution.

There are dangers in helping

Teachers are great helpers. They value that basic element of their role. Their self-esteem is fed by the recognition of their expertise as subject specialists and their caring for the young. With so many needing so much care in an age where rapid social change is creating much stress, it is easy for the teacher to see the caring role as dominant. Children cannot learn until their survival and security needs are met. Schools provide a social and success arena where children can achieve self-actualization. It is every teacher's wish for schooling to give this gift to children. To be effective in this they must help themselves by using their energy for long-term, rather than short-term, solutions.

Case Study: Tilda, 36, primary teacher

Tilda worked with many deprived children in a school which accepted children who had been refused entry elsewhere. Her vocation was to create a school world in which deprived children could feel they belonged, had worth and had competence. These were her primary goals. She had been taken off class and had a orientation role, working with newcomers who had to be assimilated into class. She gave unselfishly of her time, energy and expertise and she could not understand teachers who did not do as she did. Most of the children she had worked with were fine when she was there to support them, and because of this the Head continued to accept difficult children.

The rest of the staff admired Tilda's diligence, but they were wary of complying with her requests for help because they thought and felt differently about how help could be given. Besides, every time one pupil was settled, the next was admitted. The Head and Tilda acting as social reformers meant the staff carried a tremendous load.

One day Tilda had broken through a particular child's armour and made contact with the hurt little girl inside. She *knew* how to win the child for the school. All it needed was for the teacher to spend time one-to-one with her until the child came to trust her. She went to the teacher and asked for what she wanted:

Tilda   I need help, Maggie, with Doria. Today I found this hurt little girl inside her. She is all blast and full of fear. You must help me with her. We have the chance to save her. If you can spend 15 minutes a day with her in one-to-one, getting to know her, like I've done, in no time at all, she will come to accept school and settle down.

Maggie   I would like Doria to settle quickly. I cannot, however, give her what you have asked. I am stretched very thinly at the moment.

Tilda   Oh, Maggie, it is a hurt little girl. It would make you weep if you knew her like I do. The Head and I feel the same. We know we can ... .

It is very hard to refuse to help such appeals. The assertive teacher has to check how committing that much time, energy and expertise would detract from the educational work. A personal belief system powers this kind of evaluation. When demand exceeds supply, knowing what one values is important when organizing one's resources. If Maggie believes that providing help is an integral part of Doria's education, she will consider setting options with Tilda. If she believes that the help should come from other sources, then she must say No to the request while protecting her working relationship with Tilda.

When the demands for help exceed the capacity to comply, the assertive teacher must use all the intra- and interpersonal skills s/he possesses. Providing help at the expense of education might not be an efficient response to a problem. Society has many agencies providing help; only the school provides a structured approach to learning. If a school has a caring policy which stretches teachers too far, then they must assert their rights.

Exercises

1. Listen to couples sharing their problems and identify any of the gate-slammers or door-openers you hear.

2. Listen to a colleague moan to you about a school problem. Respond by:

Giving solutions	(Did you hear any 'yes buts'?)
Asking questions	(Did you arrive at a solution?)
Cheering them up	(Did you have success?)
Telling them about yours	(Did you shut them up?)
Reflecting their feeling	(Did you empathize?)

Ask how the person felt about your responses.

3. Intervene in a situation where your help is sought. Deliberately use the assertive skills. How did you feel when you used assertive skills? Ask those involved how they saw your intervention.

4. Read the following case study and, using the approach recommended, identify what you would do. Compare your approach with the case study's.

Case Study: Dealing with incidents

You find ten-year-old Marcia crying behind the library at lunchtime. She often cries. Her friendships are stormy and short-lived. It takes you some time to calm her down and get her to say what is the matter. She finally confesses that her friends have stopped letting her go around with them and they are calling her mother names again. It seems the new girl, Lisa, has taken charge and all Marcia's friends have turned against her.

Which option would you choose?

- You tell her not to be silly but to find some other girls to play with. You tell her to stop feeling sorry for herself.
- You give her a hug and tell her to stay by you. You chat with her about how she can win her friends back. Later you tell her teacher. Then you check with her about how things are going.
- You march her over to Lisa and co. and insist they play with her or you will tell her teacher.
- You commiserate and tell her they were not real friends and that she is better off without them. You then take her to another lonely girl and tell them to play together.
- You see her there but, because you know she cries easily and nothing does any real good, you tackle the boys who are starting to get rough with their ball play.
- You leave her there and go to find Lisa. You take Lisa aside and tell her you think she is being very unkind to Marcia and ask her to be generous and include Marcia in play.

Ten steps to success – a possible assertive approach:

1. You recognize the girl's distress and tell her you see it.
2. You comfort her and listen to her story.
3. Ask her for her solution – prompt her rather than advise her.
4. Talk with Lisa and listen only.
5. Talk with others in group to get clear picture.
6. Ask Lisa and others what Marcia has to do to be included. Prompt them to a solution.
7. Decide your next action – resolve or refer?
8. Resolve by bringing everyone together and showing how all wants can be met.
9. Refer to welfare etc. by following school procedures.
10. Follow-up to check outcome, talk with Marcia and Lisa at a later date.

In the real situation the teacher knows the 'real' Lisa and the 'real' Marcia and will decide whether to deal with them separately or to bring them together.

The assertive teacher enables those with problems to solve them under their guidance. Using two eyes to read body language, two ears to hear the words and one mouth to clarify rather than give advice, the teacher is effective. Using knowledge and experience the teacher decides when to resolve and when to refer.

6 Managing conflict

In brief

- **Conflict is inevitable.**
  Wherever teachers share resources there will be conflict.
- **Conflict is full of emotion.**
  Teachers who consistently avoid or accommodate conflict hurt themselves, their achievements and others.
- **Conflict can be managed constructively.**
  Teachers can use conflict to generate the energy they need to pursue their goals and build good relationships.
- **Conflict can be resolved without creating winners and losers.**
  Teachers with skills can resolve conflicting wants so that win-win solutions result.
- **Conflict causes an individual to take a position.**
  Teachers can choose a position appropriate to the situation.
- **Unpleasantness can be confronted pleasantly.**
  Teachers can confront the unacceptable positively.
- **Win-win outcomes require true needs to be identified.**
  Teachers who allocate time, energy and expertise to uncovering true needs find conflict can produce excellent outcomes.

Conflict is natural and inevitable

Conflict arises when teachers feel threatened in some way. The conflict can be internal or external, depending on how the teacher feels about the personal rights which are at stake.

Conflict generally has a physical effect on the body. The perceived threat causes the message to arrive at the adrenal glands that the body is threatened and immediate sugar is needed for an emergency response. The adrenals release adrenaline so that sugar can be converted to energy at high speed: the 'fight or flight' reaction. If the physical fight or flight does not occur, then the adrenaline is not readily used up. Instead, active sugar energizes the inner body and stresses it. This energy can be felt as either heat flushes of anger, or cold shivers of fear. Constant conflict which is unresolved can do great harm to the physical body and many somatic diseases reflect this. The more human beings live in confined spaces with limited resources, the greater will be the conflict and resulting stress.

Teachers see this every day in the children they teach. They see how conflict flares from 'He cussed my mum' to 'She took my pencil.' They see it in the staffroom, from 'I'm not going to do it ... I refuse ... She has no right to ask!' to 'That child has tried me too far. I am going to ....'

Conflict is full of emotion

Often the reaction to the infringement of liberty is out of all proportion to its cause. This is because the anger/fear fund is full of unspent adrenaline of previous conflicts, and one drop more causes a spill. Then the offended one, in response to an uncontrollable feeling, behaves in a way that is characteristic of the child in them rather than the adult. Adults' reactions to feelings were learned in childhood, and learning to respond to the situation instead of the feeling is an important professional step. The common belief that feelings are irrational appears true when the adult cannot separate feelings and behaviour. The premise is that it is OK to feel anger, but not to act on it without a mental process guiding it.

When others can see *virtuous* anger they tend to be sympathetic, and when they see *justified* fear they tend to be supportive. Yet when these responses have bypassed the thought processes they invariably lead to further distress. Understanding how feelings are triggered is valuable in coming to grips with the emotions that lead teachers into behaviours that are regretted later or which make matters worse.

Case Study: John, 52, primary teacher

John had a very difficult class. Never had he been able to say, 'Class stand ... Class line up ... Class sit.' Always he had to speak to individuals. There was no cohesion. This was not a group of learners, but 28 children whose need for individual attention surpassed any he had known before. He was tired, tired of teaching, tired of children, tired of looking after other people.

His widowed mother had died the previous spring and he had lived with her all his life.

One Monday morning in the staffroom he was waiting with dread for the bell to summon in the children. The bell rang and he went down to bring up his *rabble;* Hefain was back from suspension.

They made the move up the three flights of stairs in the Victorian building. At every corner Hefain flicked the child he was nearest and then bounded three more steps. John pretended not to notice. It was only Monday morning, heaven help him.

Once in the room, Hefain grabbed the seat nearest the paint racks, when he should have sat on the mat to wait for register. The others moved to the mat, but pushing and shoving to get a place with a back rest. Year 6 was grown up! Hefain was at least 5ft 8in now, taller than John.

Jonathan started to tie Billie's shoe laces together and John nudged him to stop it. Jessica started to plait Sebina's hair when she should have taken a reading book and been looking at it while awaiting dinner money collection. John asked her to collect the box for dinner money. Anwar started to cry because someone had just broken the new pencil he had brought to school. It was a normal day in 6H. But John was not normal.

When Anwar thrust the broken pencil in his face, he saw red. How dare anyone destroy a pencil. He shouted and they all cowered. All except Hefain who laughed. His mum's boyfriend shouted all the time. Out! John propelled Hefain from the room and up to the Head's room. The child was really pleased. He liked working in the corner of the Head's room and watching and listening to all that went on there.

John went back to his class, gathered his wits together, called register, collected dinner money and lined the class up for assembly. His outburst and Hefain's removal had temporarily scared the class into a compliant group. He staggered through math group-work and got to the staffroom for morning tea. He was drinking his tea when the deputy asked him to do playground duty in the absence of the rostered teacher. John exploded. He told her to take her duty and her kids and ... .

John had not dealt with his inner and outer conflicts and these had built up into a highly-pressured state. Now a minor demand on his resources had created a crisis.

The teacher under stress can be found in nearly every school, though perhaps not as extreme an example as John. Staff absentee rates reveal the teachers under stress. Both the aggressive teacher and the submissive teacher will reveal stress by their reactions to the predictable crises of school life.

School is a place where human beings are themselves, each child and adult, pursuing their own needs for recognition. Sometimes this need for recognition results in conflict. The assertive teacher deals with each conflict as it arises. A choice is made as to an appropriate response when a perceived right is infringed. A decision is made and acted upon, mistakes are made and learned from, and new directions are planned.

Conflict can be resolved without creating winners and losers

The assertive teacher does not win at the *expense* of the other. The assertive teacher wins *as well as* the other. Sometimes, winning is not an outcome and the assertive teacher only has the satisfaction of knowing that the issue was not avoided.

Case Study: Brenda, 33, primary teacher

Brenda feels she has upset Camille and the coldness between them is very uncomfortable. She is not sure how she has done it, but she suspects that it is related to parking in the school grounds. Car spaces are at a premium and they are all unnamed and filled on a first-come, first-served basis. Brenda has just started driving to school and she arrives earlier than Camille, who is always the last with a car to arrive. Probably Brenda's parking has upset Camille in some way. But this is only a guess. She decides to tackle Camille, and visits her in her classroom when the children have left.

Brenda   Hello, Camille, could we have a word?
Camille   Certainly, Brenda.
Brenda   Camille, I am feeling uncomfortable when I am near you. Is something wrong?
Camille   No, not that I know of.
Brenda   It is funny, I just feel uncomfortable and I wondered if I had done or said something that upset you. Please tell me if I have because I want to put it right. I don't like feeling this way.
Camille   I don't know what you are talking about, Brenda.
Brenda   Well, I am glad about that.

Two days later Brenda heard from a colleague that Camille was angry with her because her car had been scraped while parked in the road outside the school, because Brenda had taken Camille's car space. Brenda seeks out Camille again in her classroom after school.

Brenda   Camille, I feel that you are angry with me and you were not willing to tell me so the other day. Let's talk about it.

Camille   I am angry, but it's not your fault and yet I blame you.

Brenda   Go on.

Camille   Since you have been bringing your car, I have had to park out in the street. That made me angry because I am always rushing and late and of course I had to carry loads of stuff in.

Brenda   Go on.

Camille   Well, yesterday when I went to my car, someone had broken off the aerial to the radio and, well, Jim will be furious with me when he hears.

Brenda   (Is silent.)

Camille   Well, I know it is not your fault but I do blame you because if you had not brought your car in, it would not have happened.

Brenda   I know about irrational anger. I can see that what you say is true. I do have equal rights with you to park in the grounds. Yet I understand you are angry at whoever broke your aerial, at yourself for being too rushed to lower it, and that you are scared of the trouble when you tell Jim.

Camille   Yes. If you were not bringing your car, it would not have happened.

Brenda   True.

Camille   (Is silent.)

Brenda   What do you need me to do so that you are not angry at me?

Camille   Oh, I'll get over it once I have a lashing from Jim.

Brenda   Camille, why don't you go to Jim and say, 'Jim, someone has snapped off the aerial on the car. What will WE do about it?' If he shouts at you, say 'Jim, I do not like you shouting at me as if I was a naughty child. Please stop.'

Camille   You don't know Jim.

Brenda   Just try it. You will feel better for saying it no matter what he does.

Brenda checks the next day to see how Camille managed Jim.

What has Brenda done? She has acted on her bad feelings and admitted them openly to Camille. At first, when Camille was not prepared to co-operate in resolving the situation, Brenda just accepted the answer, even though she still felt there was something wrong. In acting on her feelings she did the assertive thing. It did not work, but that does not matter because she knows she has done her best to confront the situation.

When her feelings are later confirmed with hearsay, she did not dive off to Camille with an accusation. She waited until the day's task was done and then went to find Camille. Place and time are important: their conversation was held in private without infringing on other staff. It gave Brenda time to distance herself from the feelings of anger she had about Camille and to be responsible by not letting a personal issue interfere with the working day.

In the second conversation, Brenda is more direct without accusing Camille of anything. Brenda does not want to cast blame or make Camille feel bad. She wants the bad feelings removed. The assertive person is not interested in laying blame, shame or guilt on anyone. S/he wants conflict to be resolved so that good relationships result and work goals can be pursued without negative interference.

Brenda does not put words into Camille's mouth or give her information to prompt her. She simply says 'go on ... '. When she has heard enough, she summarizes what she has heard and accepts Camille's feelings as true for her if not for the situation. She then volunteers an assertive way for Camille to manage the anger of Jim.

Brenda is fully co-operative and fully determined to solve the feeling problem between them. Her feelings are stated rather than shown, and even though she had *given up* she had returned to the problem when it resurfaced.

Taking a position in a conflict situation

The assertive teacher has strategies for managing the trigger feelings and then choosing a position. The positions range from ignoring unacceptable behaviour from another or exploding with rage (real or pretended), to smoothing over and submitting to please or bargaining. The best position is to come to a resolution with the other, using assertive strategies.

John ignored irritations and then exploded. This is a common way for non-assertive people to behave. The last straw for the submissive and the guilt of the aggressive pushes them from one extreme to another. John's behaviour is working against him. Assertiveness is about becoming centred, with feelings and behaviour working for the person instead of against them. Brenda responded to a situation with open honesty and no ulterior motives. She admitted her feelings. She acted on her feelings and her behaviour worked for her. All teachers can learn how to do this. Then they can choose. To ignore or to fire or to resolve: these are identifiable skills.

Conflict resolved with skill does not need to use power

The skills of managing conflict include:

   feeling the feeling and identifying it

separating the feeling from the behaviour
stating the feeling
giving an *I do not* ... message
defining the conflict without blame being involved
identifying the real issues in terms of outcomes wanted
generating possible solutions
negotiating acceptable solutions
checking outcome satisfaction.

Case Study: Tom, 38, Deputy Head, secondary school

Tom felt the staff was basically lazy and that he had to watch them closely and keep them on task. Standards had to be lifted and much of that depended on his ensuring that the staff did their best at all times. There were three teachers he was particularly worried about: Selia, 23, newly out of training and too easy on the kids; Felicia, 34, a young mother with a lot of absenteeism, and Brandy, 45 and cynical about the whole of education.

He tackled Selia first. He called her to his office in a non-teaching period and his frustration with her was obvious from his curt behaviour towards her. Selia was stunned at first but she hid her hurt from Tom.

Tom   Selia, it just won't do, you are letting the kids walk all over you. You'll have to do better than that, you know. What I want you to do is get tough with them. Don't stand for any trouble or backchat. Just stop being so nice to them. They're here to work, not play.

Selia   What?

Tom   You heard me, the behaviour of your classes is not good enough. You have to change that.

Selia   How do I do that?

Tom   That is your problem.

Selia   Yes, Tom, but I need some back-up.

Tom   Just send them to me if they won't do as you say. But say it and mean it!

Tom's abrupt beginning stuns Selia and she has to fight off feelings of either distress or anger. By an effort of will she manages to sound calm. Tom's blaming messages push Selia into a *yes but* mode. He has given her an instruction and a quick solution to the problem. Selia will probably go back to her students, shout at the first one who steps out of line, and send him or her to Tom and further lose the respect of her students. Tom has not considered the situation from her point of view. He has given the issue little time and is not enabling Selia to improve by rescuing her with a send-them-to-me solution.

An assertive deputy would go with the problem to Selia and after saying how he felt about Selia's management of the students, ask what she needed to reduce the unacceptable behaviour of some of her students. Together they would identify a way for Selia to implement a get-tough style. The language would be inclusive, full of *I*s and *we*s and *our*s. Quieter classes would be the outcome.

An assertive Selia would clarify the complaint and then ask for what she wanted when the deputy found her style wanting.

Selia	I feel hurt by your comments, Tom. Could you give me some examples of where I have been too soft, Tom?
Tom	Well, the noise from the showers is dreadful and I heard the way Sally spoke to you which was appalling.
Selia	So you want my classes to be quieter in the showers and you want me to correct the way some students speak to me.
Tom	That will be a start.
Selia	I will need some support.
Tom	You are trained; you should know how to do it.
Selia	I will need some support, Tom.
Tom	What do you mean?
Selia	I will need support from you. I think it would be a good idea if you come to the start of each of my lessons next week and I speak to them about the noise levels while you watch, and I tell them that if they are not quiet for me, you and I will have to find a way to reduce the noise. Then they will see I have the power and your support.
Tom	OK, we will see if that works.

Selia knew her control tactics were poor and she wanted Tom to be specific about particular areas of her control so that she could identify solutions with him. She used 'broken record' – *I will need some support* – to Tom's resistance to her request for help, and then she worked out how she could use Tom's position to gain some power back to make her classes quieter. She will need to find a way of correcting rudeness from a student. The standard, 'I do not like the way you are speaking to me. Please don't,' will work in a majority of cases.

Generally it only needs one person to be assertive to get a decent solution. There are occasions where one person's bull-headedness prevents the assertive person getting anywhere. In that case, the only satisfaction for the assertive one is knowing that they have done their best.

Felicia has had another day off school, nearly all her leave has been used and the rest of the staff have had to cover because all leave has been in a no-supply-cover category of odd hours and half-days. Tom awaits her arrival the next morning. He asks her to come into his office where he tells her she is not giving enough to her job. She bursts into tears and leaves his office, goes to her car and drives back home. Tom feels dreadful or Tom feels furious with her. It does not matter which, his feeling level is up and will affect his efficiency that day. An assertive Tom would have dealt with the situation later in the day and in Felicia's territory.

Tom	Felicia, is it all right for us to have a word? I have been worried about you.
Felicia	Yes, Tom, but I have only five minutes as I must get home quickly.
Tom	I know that you are having some problems with the family and it is making demands on your time. Would you like to tell me about it?
Felicia	Well, the baby is having digestive troubles, and Milly is very jealous of the new baby, and my husband cannot cope because he cannot sleep during the day.
Tom	He works night shift, doesn't he?
Felicia	That's right, and normally he can manage enough sleep if the children are OK.
Tom	You have a problem, Felicia, and that gives me a problem, because I have to keep covering your classes. Your duties are pulling you in opposite directions.
Felicia	Well, I cannot help that. I am entitled to leave and I have to give my babies priority.
Tom	I understand your predicament, but I still have to cover for you and explain to staff why they must do more than their share of work.
Felicia	That's your job.
Tom	How do you suggest I handle it?
Felicia	I don't know. I have enough on my plate.
Tom	You may have to ask for leave without pay if you need more time to settle the children. I could speak to the governors for you.
Felicia	Oh, we have to have the money coming in.
Tom	Well, I will have to ask you to think about how you can manage to keep your contract with us. Please give some thought as to how you can provide for your children's care while being here at school. I will check with you tomorrow after you have talked with your husband.

Here, Tom has accepted that Felicia has a problem and kept her onside. He has given her no excuse to flounce off or lift his emotional level. He has not blamed her for anything; he has merely identified the problem and invited her to give a solution, resourcing it with limited time. Tomorrow he must have a solution in case she has not one or it is unacceptable. Legal solutions may be necessary if creative ones are not forthcoming.

Brandy has been alienating some of his students with his cynical attitude to life and education. Tom has had to speak with him a few times about some of the statements he has used in class. One or two parents have been in to the Head asking for their children to be changed to another class. Tom hates this side of his job; disciplining staff really gets him edgy. He now has to confront Brandy and he sends a note asking Brandy to come to his office in his non-teaching period one afternoon. An assertive Tom would practise deep breathing and do some meditation to get himself ready.

Then . . .

Brandy	You wanted to see me, Tom?
Tom	Yes, Brandy, we have a problem with your 3B. I feel very awkward about having to speak to you about this. Have a seat.
Brandy	Thanks. Will this take long? I have to get things ready for next lesson.
Tom	I hope not. I too have a class next period. I said we had a problem, Brandy. It's a big tough one. Two parents of students in 3B have been to the Head to ask for their children to be removed from your class because they do not like the attitude you have to your subject.
Brandy	Oh, that's a load of garbage, Tom. They must have it in for me, for some reason. Is it young Holt and his cronies, Nilson and Bright? They are dissatisfied with the marks they got in the last test.
Tom	No, Brandy, it's not them. You and I have spoken before about how your view of things is interfering with your teaching. Now we have parents lodging complaints and we have to go a step further. If we do not relocate the students, they will take the case to the governors.
Brandy	Well, do what you must. I have done nothing wrong. This parent power is stupid, what do they know? It is ridiculous.
Tom	Removing the students solves the parent's problems but it creates new problems for the school, Brandy. How can I be sure more parents won't arrive with similar complaints? I will have to organize an investigation into your teaching. I warned you

	earlier that you needed to be careful and you assured me that you had everything under control. How do you feel about that?
Brandy	I am sure this is a set-up, Tom … let me talk with the kids or their parents.
Tom	Well, one solution is to have a meeting with the students, parents and us – let me take the idea to the Head. It will be testing. The real problem is that the parents have given a solution which we have to implement, but in implementing it we create another problem. That is, how do we stop such complaints in future?

The assertive Tom prepared himself for a task he hated by a routine relaxation technique. He knew he had a tendency to believe the staff were lazy, and knowing this has given him some control over letting it interfere with a best way of managing a confrontation. In this, he recognized that his feelings of anxiety might interfere with his ability to be objective so he thought out what he wanted to say before Brandy arrived. He said he felt awkward. He identified the problem and made no blaming statements. He had an idea of an acceptable outcome, which was to respond to the parents' request either by removing the students or by setting up a group to arrive at an alternative acceptable solution. The longer-term problem is to help Brandy change his cynicism or leave the profession. Separating the two issues is important in getting the best solutions to both.

Tom can become assertive in these three examples. He can find a way to manage the feelings that he has prior to a confrontation and define the conflict without blaming anyone. He can learn to see real issues and separate them and he can put into practice the idea of letting the person who caused the conflict contribute to the conflict's solutions. This will make him more flexible and more able to move between positions. He will keep good relationships even while having to criticize.

Case Study: Frances, 22, primary teacher, first year

Frances was working quietly in a corner of the staffroom when Mr Cannon, the chair of governors, entered the room with Stella and Bob. Stella was a meal supervisor and Bob was a teacher, psychologically retired and in his last year of service. Frances and Bob got on well.

The three newcomers did not notice Frances and they were obviously heated by the behaviour of Frazer, a difficult pupil to handle. Bob was saying that he could not tolerate Frazer any more as he had kicked Stella, called her a bloody bitch and then threatened him with a chair. He demanded that the governor suspend the *black basted* and lay it on the line to the Head who was sure to defend Frazer because she was soft on blacks. Stella added that the school had gone downhill since black students became the majority. Frances had to make a decision. Should she stay hidden or should she speak up? Should she ignore the comments or protest?

Frances's options are many. She can:

- Keep quiet and hope they leave and then pretend nothing happened.
- Keep quiet and then go to the Head with a report and an objection.
- Emerge, give them all a dirty look and then leave.
- Emerge, tell them they are racist bigots and that she will report them.
- Emerge, commiserate and agree that Frazer is too much.
- Emerge, say how she feels about the exchange. Point out that Frazer's behaviour is his own and not a whole race's behaviour.

Frances can respond emotionally and be at the mercy of what happens next. Or, she can feel the feeling and publicly own it: 'I am shocked at what I have heard.' She can then explain her position: 'Frazer is difficult, I agree. What I have just heard makes me realize that you are attributing his behaviour to all blacks and I do not like that.' She can ask for what she wants: 'I would like an apology.'

She can report the incident as a racist incident if she wants to punish the offenders or make a public case of the incident for political reasons. She has a right to do that. She also has a responsibility as a professional teacher to preserve the image of teachers. If she can keep the matter in-house and ensure that the offenders are challenged and given an opportunity to resolve/learn from the experience, then she has a win-win solution. Frances can want to punish the offenders for the hurt they have caused her or she can want to change their behaviour.

The issue of racism within the school context is sensitive. Sometimes the anger that is triggered by a racist comment or act is anger stored from many previous situations. Inner conflict often determines the outer manifestation of that conflict: either paralysis or over-reaction.

An assertive Frances would emerge and state how she feels about what she has heard. She will trust the system to support her even in her junior status as she faces the chair of governors. A non-assertive Frances would either injure herself by over-reacting and being aggressive or injure herself by passively ignoring the incident.

Assertiveness has costs as well as benefits. The assertive person does come from a position of strength. The assertive person can manage the feelings and choose how to respond. The non-assertive person fires from the hip with a response that is fuelled by feeling. However, the assertive person must learn how to resist the feeling imperative and give up revenge as a strategy.

Conflict resolution needs skill to be done without unpleasantness

The essential rule for any conflict confrontation which is very important is to protect the relationship while pursuing a quality outcome. This needs skill. The skill is in identifying the real issue and using the expertise of staff to generate enough potential solutions so that all with a stake in the outcome can be satisfied. Quality solutions are needed when implementation depends on the willingness of staff. Pleasing everyone with a quality response is not easy, but it is not impossible.

When a problem is ignored or avoided, there is no attempt to protect a relationship or to move to a solution. Sometimes problems do go away without having to be addressed, but if this is a teacher's preferred solution, then job satisfaction is low and poor relationships result.

When a problem solution is designed only in relation to a desired outcome and the relationship is seen as unimportant, then a highly competitive style will get some short-term job satisfaction but will alienate colleagues in the long term. If this is a teacher's pattern then teamwork is virtually impossible. Collaboration is essential these days if quality outcomes are to be achieved.

When a problem solution is designed to keep people happy, then standards are sacrificed to relationships. Happy environments can produce comfort zones which interfere with quality being pursued. Goals are sacrificed to keep the peace. When a teacher operates in this style, achievement is substandard and people become threatened by outside critics.

When a problem solution is always a trade-off, bargaining with people and compromising goals, then some satisfactions are achieved but quality outcomes and quality relationships are elusive. Though it may seem fair, when a teacher has only this style of managing conflict true satisfaction is never experienced. What is fair is not always the best solution in a conflict.

An example of this is the story about the mother who saw her twin girls fighting over one orange. She took charge and divided the orange in two. One girl went to the squeezer and extracted the juice and drank it, then put the rind in the bin. The other girl went to the grater, grated the rind for an orange cake and put the pulp in the bin. One girl could have had all the pulp and the other all the rind. Uncovering the real need is important when there is conflict over resources.

Win-win conflict resolution needs a clear understanding of what the true needs are

When real needs are uncovered it is possible to create win-win outcomes which create high satisfaction for all people. The win-win outcome demands time, energy, expertise and a desire to co-operate. When a problem solution aims for a quality outcome and good relationships, then time must be found, though not every problem needs a quality solution or the satisfaction of all parties.

In order to achieve quality conflict solutions, teachers must invest time, energy and expertise in first identifying the real issues, and then involving the right people, both in generating enough satisfactory outcomes, and in evaluating selected outcomes. The selected solution must be well-resourced and implemented. If all this is done properly, everyone who has a stake in the outcome will be satisfied.

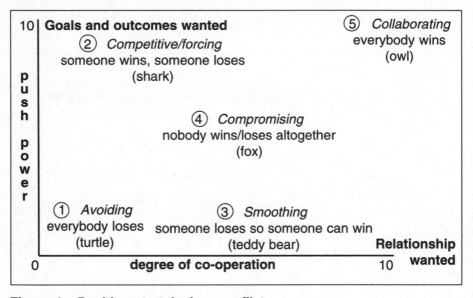

Figure 1   Positions to take in a conflict
Source: animals from David W. Johnson (1986), *Reaching Out*, Englewood, NJ: Prentice-Hall.

Imagine this is a graph and you have scored five people according to how much power they have used (on the vertical) in a situation and how co-operative they have been with another (on the horizontal) when they resolve a conflict.

- At Position 1 is someone who hates conflict of any kind and who keeps a low profile whenever there is a difference of opinion. This person would rather give up what is wanted and stay out of the way of the other, than deal with that difference. Avoidance is the behaviour.
- At Position 2 is someone who relishes conflict and loves to compete and force the opposition to give in. This person sacrifices relationships and people's feelings in the name of goals and achievement. Forcing is the behaviour.
- At Position 3 is someone who dislikes difference and opposition so much that whatever is wanted is given up so that the other can have want s/he wants. This person believes conflict to be destructive of relationships. Smoothing is the behaviour.
- At Position 4 is someone who believes that in life there is never enough for everyone to have what they want, so compromise is always necessary. S/he exerts some effort towards a resolution of difference and tries to keep the other happy. Compromising is the behaviour.
- At Position 5 is someone who believes that it is important and possible to pursue goals and work with the other to make sure that both are satisfied with the outcomes. S/he wants the conflict to be constructive. Such behaviour is collaborating.

Most teachers take all of these positions at one time or another. The assertive teacher can choose a position which is situationally appropriate. The professional teacher can successfully use all the positions in Figure 1. Choice is available. For example, it is OK to ignore some problems when the goal is not important, the relationship is not important, and time is short. It is OK to push with personal power when the goal is very important and the relationship with others is not important and time is limited. When the relationship is very important, the outcome is not, and time is limited, it is OK to give up the goal and co-operate fully with another. When both relationship and outcome are equally important and time is limited, it is OK to exert some push and be partly co-operative. However, when the goal is very important and the relationship is very important, then time must be found to arrive at a win-win solution.

Winners who create losers generally create a backlash, so it is essential to either keep people onside or make a decision which is outside their area of concern. Losers who create winners generally grow resentful eventually, so it is essential for them to identify where their primary goals must take precedence over others' needs.

All positions are useful and the idea that teachers have choice is empowering. Choosing to avoid is different from avoiding automatically; choosing to co-operate or push ahead empowers similarly. Choosing to compromise rather than believing one always has to give up part of what is wanted is empowering. Personal power is increased by choice and increases the number of win-win outcomes.

Believing that there is enough for everyone can be quite difficult when the current practice is competition for scarce resources. Teachers must be involved in planning because when they have access to the whole picture they can see where goals and relationships contribute to job satisfaction. The school process, then, must accept that teachers have expertise and a stake in reaching quality goals, with conflict providing power push to achieve them.

Teachers in schools need to contribute to the school mission statement and identify where their practice contributes to the achievement of the objectives. They can then prepare their needs for resources and see where they fit in the whole. Designing their own programme budget in line with negotiated priorities can determine time-lines for the achievement of goals. Recognizing where teamwork is essential to quality outcomes, assertive teachers will contribute with a balance of power push and co-operation.

Exercises

1. Are you a shark, fox, turtle, teddy bear or owl?

    When?
    Where?
    Why?
    Self-analysis, reflection and acceptance.

2. Remember three occasions where you were in conflict with another.

    Did you win? lose?
    Did the other(s) lose or win?
    Did you create a win-win situation?
    Did you push for your own wants and be blowed to the other people? (Shark goes for the kill.)
    Did you give up what you wanted to keep the peace? (Teddy bear smoothes the conflict away.)
    Did you ignore the issue as too testing? (Turtle pulls its head in.)
    Did you give a bit to get a bit? (Fox bargains and compromises so that there are no losses.)
    Did you all end up happy with a quality solution? (Owl achieves win-win solutions.)

3. How would each animal deal with the following?

    a. Respond to another teacher bawling out their noisy class?
    b. Reject a parent's request for extra work for their child?
    c. Accept a colleague's request to do duty?
    d. Receive a delegated unpopular task?

Possible answers to Exercise 3:

a. Teachers bawling out the class

Shark	How dare you talk to my class that way!
Teddy bear	Oh dear, have they been too noisy?
Turtle	Books out, 3b.
Fox	Right, you've been noisy, Miss X will speak to you at playtime.
Owl	I feel sad that you have had to speak to my class and disappointed that you have been noisy enough to draw attention to yourselves.

b. Parent request

Shark	That is too much. I have far too much to do too!
Teddy bear	Oh well, I suppose I can fit it in somewhere.
Turtle	Let's not talk about it now, I'm busy.
Fox	Well, you come in and we can do it together.
Owl	He needs that extra work. I suggest I send you some suggestions each evening.

c. Colleague request

Shark	Bloody hell, definitely NO!
Teddy bear	Oh well, why not? I do it for everybody else.
Turtle	(Do not hear and move away.)
Fox	If you take Dannie while I go swimming.
Owl	If it is essential and you can find no-one else, I will, but I will expect you to owe me a duty.

d. Delegated request

Shark	Get lost. Ask Jane!
Teddy bear	Oh, is it my turn? I cannot do it this time but I will next.
Turtle	OK (and then not do it, take the consequences).
Fox	What's in it for me if I do it? I want ... .
Owl	I do not want to do this. I will, but please do not ask me again until everyone has had a turn.

Choosing wisely in each situation means that each teacher can earn a reputation for flexibility and consistency. Each is able to respond appropriately after checking with feelings and thoughts, anticipating outcomes, and contributing to good staff relations and the achievement of quality goals.

7 Giving and receiving feedback

In brief

- **Feedback is essential if effectiveness is to be increased.**
  Teachers receive feedback from students, peers and managers informally and formally.
- **Feedback can be given destructively or constructively.**
  Teachers can be wounded or inspired by feedback.
- **Constructive feedback comes as praise and criticism.**
  Teachers can give and receive praise and criticism with skill. Teachers who manage a no-blame feedback process are valuable colleagues.
- **Feedback received must be assessed.**
  Feedback often has a value judgement attached to it. Teachers must judge the veracity and value of feedback after considering the motive of the giver.

Feedback is essential

Feedback is any information received by a teacher on how they were received by another. It comes from pupils, students, colleagues, managers, parents, governors and just about anybody who ever went to school. Everyone appears to be an expert on the teacher's performance! That can be a problem for teachers when morale is low; everyone's criticism seems significant.

Feedback often comes as praise and/or criticism, frequently with the giver's approval or disapproval attached. Feedback that is information without the giver's judgement allows the actor to apply their own judgement criteria. Feedback that is information of an evaluative nature is most valuable when given as an *I* message. The assertive teacher gives information with an *I feel* message which shows the effect of something on them. The best way to give feedback is to give it as a description of how an action was received by a person rather than as an evaluative comment, the exception being where the feedback is a measure of achievement against some objective criteria.

Some people see the world pessimistically and look for the things that are below standard. Others see the world optimistically and look for the things that are rewarding. At its worst, the Pollyanna view becomes a denial of reality, but at its best it makes the world a better place to be.

For example, a picnic in the country planned for a June day is eagerly anticipated. The day dawns wet and windy. The pessimist says, 'I told you so, the picnic is ruined.' The optimist says, 'What a pity we cannot have our picnic outdoors; we will have it inside.' The realist, in the UK, plans for a summer or winter day approach to a picnic and the alternative plans are both rewarding.

Feedback can be given destructively or constructively

Pessimists and optimists can both give and receive feedback destructively or constructively. Criticism is generally comment which finds fault with something, and it can be done constructively. Praise is generally comment which commends something, though even this can be done destructively. This is because of a tendency to undermine a piece of praise with a *but*, and soften a piece of criticism with a *but*. It also is reinforced or undermined by body language or tone and inflection. When the words are not congruent with the body language, gesture and tone, then people believe the body language. It is harder to lie with the body language which tends to reveal feeling, while the words reveal the thoughts.

As a general rule, feedback is effective when it enables the receiver to use it to advantage. The way it is given affects how it is received.

Case Study: Annie, 31, primary teacher

Annie was very hardworking. She set very high standards for herself and for others and she was not backwards in speaking her mind. Whenever she gave criticism her voice rose, and when she gave praise, which was seldom, she squirmed and avoided eye contact.

With her pupils, she always balanced praise with criticism, giving with one hand and taking back with the other, for example, 'You have a very good story here, but look at the handwriting! You described the kitten so wonderfully, then you made three spelling mistakes' or 'Jack, you walked in so quietly yesterday, but today, you have forgotten your manners.'

With her colleagues she had a tendency to generalize: 'Barbara, could you get here earlier? You always keep us waiting when we go to swimming' or 'Colin, you never ask if I could help and I could do that for you.' She undermined her comments with general statements such as 'always' and 'never' with which people could easily argue.

With seniors and authority she always preceded feedback with an apology, such as 'Excuse me, Mr Groves, that isn't strictly true. I did not say that' or 'I am sorry to say that I will not be able to help then.' As a result, she generally sounded as if she was making excuses rather than having made decisions.

With everyone, she applied her own high standards and she was critical of anything less than perfect: 'That display should have had a border and then it would have looked more professional' or 'If that question had been asked at the meeting we would not be in this fix now' or 'People just don't try hard enough these days. It is all so slap-dash.' With these kinds of statements, she alienated people by her focus on what should have been rather than what was.

People tended to avoid giving her feedback, because it involved them in too much debate. When feedback did come her way she tended to argue with it and defend her position quite fervently. If she started to lose an argument she said, 'Well, anyway . . . ' and changed the topic. This meant that she did not learn much about how she was received, and her behaviour went unchanged.

After attending a seminar on Performance Appraisal, the Head saw a way to raise the question of feedback as part of the process. She spoke to Annie informally before the process was to begin:

Head   Annie, I want us to talk about the process of feedback and the purpose of Performance Appraisal. I have decided to have a word with each staff member privately rather than bring up the points in a staff meeting, because I think we will all benefit from practising the process, at least at a feeling level. So this is an informal practice of a formal process. Is that OK with you?

Annie   If you think that is necessary, Head.

Head   I do. Now the whole process of appraisal is about communication. It is an opportunity for you and I to have a formal conversation about how we work together. I think we will talk about feedback and how we give and receive it. There will be some seminars on it and you might choose to go to one. Or we might each choose a topic, research it and present a short

	talk in staff meeting on it. What do we agree feedback to be?
Annie	Well, I think it is telling someone what their strengths and weaknesses are. We have always done that with the pupils and now we are going to do it as an inspection technique!
Head	I think it is telling others how they are received by us or how they reach certain objective criteria. And yes, I agree, it is becoming part of an inspection process. So I think we need to have certain rules about how we do that. I thought you and I might focus on those and present the rules in staff meeting as a model for the others. The option would be to go to a seminar and be told, but as you know that is an expensive drain on the staff development budget. What do you think?

The Head has raised the element of feedback with a staff member who has a lot to learn about it. She has given Annie a limited choice. The Head could have sent for her and told her that she needed to improve the way she gave praise and criticism. Annie would have argued, or pretended to agree and then done nothing on one excuse or another as a response to this approach. Giving direct feedback like this is fine, once staff morale is high and the school climate is one in which direct feedback functioning in a no-blame way is the norm. Until that is the case, a Head must find individual strategies that work with individuals. She has used the idea of the Appraisal and she must use this with every staff member if Annie is not to see the method as manipulation.

Annie's task is to acquire the skills of giving feedback. She will need to identify people's motives in giving feedback and this will influence the style in which it is given. When people honestly acknowledge to themselves their motives they become much more open and honest with themselves and others, and trust improves.

Constructive feedback comes as praise and criticism

Giving feedback: Praise

Decide why you are giving praise.

- To make the person feel good.
- To show your appreciation.
- To identify what you like.
- To commend achievement.

Praise the deed and the person, using their name.

- 'Thank you for bringing up my class today, Preyma. I really appreciate your thoughtfulness' rather than 'You're a good person for bringing them up.'
- 'I really appreciate your thoughtfulness in tidying the paint corner, Jenny. Thank you' rather than 'Thanks for being helpful.'

Be particular.

- 'That was excellently executed. I particularly liked the way you asked us to check our answers with a partner before you asked us to give them to the whole floor, Patrick' rather than 'You are such a good teacher.'
- 'That display looks excellent, Sabina. I think it is the bordering that sets it off' rather than 'Well done, you always do excellent displays.'

Try to match the praise to the person's value system.

- 'What an excellent meal! You treat your guests so well, Sarah' rather than 'I envy you. You are a good cook.'
- 'Those colours go so well together. I admire your taste, Bryan' rather than 'That looks nice.'

Identify the good *bit so that the person can repeat it.*

- 'Adrian, you spoke so clearly. I have heard you many times speak to parents and I find the way you introduce us so effective. You capture each of us precisely in a few words' rather than 'You're so good at introducing people.'
- 'I like your hair. It looks stunning, Nan. That cut suits you' rather than 'Your hair looks nice today.'

NB: Personal comments should only be given in response to a request or when the giver is in a relationship where such feedback is part of a relationship.

Giving feedback: Criticism

Decide why you are giving the criticism.

- To make the person feel bad.

- To stop a behaviour.
- To have the person make amends.
- To improve performance.

Give an I message not a you message.

- 'I find your talking when I am talking very distracting and I cannot teach Anne' rather than 'You are a chatterbox and thoughtless. You are not being fair to Anne.'
- 'I found the noise of your class very disturbing today' rather than 'Your lot were rowdy today.'

Criticize the deed, not the person.

- 'Spilling that water was the result of your not exercising enough care' rather than 'You stupid, careless idiot!'
- 'Those shoes are not good for the walk we will have to do today. What can we do?' rather than 'Only a fool would think those shoes would do today.'

Reveal your feelings.

- 'I feel very angry when you ask me to do extra duty' rather than '... mutter mutter ... '
- 'I get very frustrated when staff meeting goes beyond 4:30 and I become agitated' rather than 'I'm leaving at 4:30 finished or not!'

Describe the tangible effects of that which has prompted you to criticize.

- 'When you take your class to the video room without checking the booking sheet, I waste a lot of time waiting for you to move out again' rather than 'You should check the video room bookings before wasting my time.'
- 'I was unable to complete my marking because I had to do your hour of invigilation when you forgot yesterday' rather than 'Your poor memory messed me up yesterday.'

Say what you want instead of condemning what occurred.

- 'I would like you to check with me before you do any more photocopying' rather than 'You shouldn't photocopy without permission.'
- 'I want your class to move quietly past my room on their way to

gym' rather than 'Keep your class quiet, for goodness sake!'

Receiving feedback: Criticism

Check the veracity of the feedback.

- If it is true, receive it graciously.
- If it is untrue, receive it and say you cannot agree because ....
- If you are unsure, say ' You may be right' or 'I will think about that and get back to you.'

Check the motive of the critic.

If you are unsure,	ask for their motive; say you are unsure of why they are speaking.
If it is to make you feel bad,	say you are angry at the person for wanting to make you feel bad.
If it is a put-down, challenge it:	is that a put-down? did you mean to put me down?
If it is to guide you to better ways,	thank them for their concern; say you appreciate their advice.

Receive the message.

- 'I hear what you say and I think it is not good to say it' rather than 'Don't say that.'
- 'Thank you for telling me that but I would prefer you not to repeat it' rather than 'You should not say things like that.'
- 'It is interesting that you should think that' rather than 'I disagree.'

Say how the feedback makes you feel.

- 'I feel hurt that you should want to tell me that' rather than 'That's cruel of you.'
- 'I am angry that you should take her comments about me as true' rather than 'You are as bad as her.'
- 'I am surprised you would think that of me' rather than 'And you believe that!'

Say what you think they are feeling.

- 'You sound fed up with me' rather than 'You disapprove.'
- 'You are frightened that I would not include you, so you are saying ...' rather than 'You think I missed you out.'
- 'You sound delighted to have found me out' rather than 'You think it clever to have caught me out.'

Confirm feedback which you meant to give.

- 'Yes, I did criticize the performance. I am sorry you only heard what I did not like' rather than 'Oh! I said loads of good things too.'
- 'Yes, I did say that I found your habit of arriving late annoying. I should have told you before I told anyone else. I apologize' rather than 'Well, you are always late.'
- 'I was telling Angela how much I enjoyed your assembly the other day' rather than 'We liked your assembly yesterday.'

Ask what you can do to make amends.

- 'You are distressed because I did that, what can I do to make it up to you?' rather than 'It won't happen again.'
- 'I regret that. Can I correct it?' rather than 'I'm sorry, I'll make it up to you.'
- 'I am sorry you feel that way. Please accept my apology' rather than 'Oh, that was silly of me, will you forgive me?'

Challenge the untrue or ulterior motive.

- 'I wonder why you would say that' rather than 'You must be mad to say that about me.'
- 'Ouch, that feels like a put-down. Did you mean it to be?' rather than 'And the same to you!'
- 'That is an untrue statement and I want you to retract it' rather than 'That's a horrid thing to say.'

Receiving feedback: Praise

Always receive praise graciously, even when you suspect the motive.

- 'Thank you for your comments, Maria' rather than 'What!'

- 'How kind of you to say so, Balwart' rather than 'You like this old thing?'

NB: Do not think you must return a compliment with a compliment.

Feedback received and assessed can be valuable recognition

One of the most important motivators of teachers is recognition. They value hard work and they like to be recognized for both effort and achievement. Feedback is therefore of utmost importance, particularly when cuts in education limit the promotion opportunities which are the most outward reward of excellence in the system. Payment by results is more a threat than a promise to teachers who see examination results as only one element of success from teaching. Performance Appraisal is yet another threat rather than opportunity when it is linked to promotion and pay, rather than just personal development towards excellence.

Teachers need to know how they are doing. They value feedback from parents, pupils, students and colleagues as well as from the system itself. The assertive teacher is a colleague who provides information that guides a teacher towards greater achievement. Giving genuine responses to the way a teacher demonstrates their talents is a valuable way of developing them. Being open to feedback is a valuable way of reflecting on one's performance and redirecting one's efforts. High self-esteem teachers risk being open to feedback from those they have decided are significant.

Case Study: Merran, 29, PE teacher

Merran had a knack of getting the best from people, whether they were students, parents or teachers. She spoke openly to all as if they were guests in her time and space. She listened more than she spoke. When a student nearly knocked her over in a corridor and kept on running she sought him out later and said,

Merran	Paul, at lunch time today I felt badly shaken when you raced past me and I lost my balance. (She establishes eye contact and maintains silence, awaiting Paul's response.)
Paul	Sorry, miss.
Merran	How can I be sure that it won't happen again? (She maintains eye contact and silence.)
Paul	I don't know, miss.

Merran	I want you to walk at all times in the corridors.
Paul	Yes, miss. (She finalizes Paul's agreement.)
Merran	What do I want, Paul? (Still keeping eye contact and silence until Paul speaks.)
Paul	You want me to always walk in the corridors.
Merran	Can you do that?
Paul	Yes.
Merran	OK, I'll check that in the next few weeks and see if you meant it.

This is a *no blame* piece of criticism. In terms of time commitment, it is expensive in the short term, but cheap in the long term. It means that Merran must earn herself a reputation for giving feedback that leaves a person enough room to make amends without having bad feelings.

To do this you have to believe in the right of everyone to receive polite interactions. It means you have to control the feelings that you feel like showing. You can do this by stating the feeling instead of showing it. Merran did this with Paul when she said she was badly shaken.

Paul was co-operative. However, it worked for Merran with unco-operative people, too. Cal Fischer was the school keeper. He was making heavy work of fixing some lockers to a wall near the gym. The noise of his hammering and cursing was disrupting Merran's movement-to-music class, so she went out to ask if he could delay the work until the last few students had finished their assessment piece.

Merran	Cal, the noise of your work is making it impossible for me to finish my lesson. Could you stop for a while?
Cal	No way. The Head said I had to have this done before lunch as visitors this afternoon will want to inspect the provision for year four to store their gear.
Merran	Cal, I really would be pleased if you could halt for just 15 minutes while three students do their pieces.
Cal	You heard me. I have to get it finished.
Merran	Look, Cal. My girls need the quietness. What can I do that will allow you to wait 15 minutes?
Cal	Nothing.
Merran	If I come and hold them in place for you as soon as they've finished, you can still have them finished before lunch. Your co-operation would enable the girls to have their results today, and when they know you did that they will have you to thank for shortening their suspense.

Merran has played the last card she has. If Cal values the opinions of the students he will co-operate. Merran might have said that she would tell the

Head how co-operative he has been if she thought he valued the Head's opinion. If he is just plain awkward, then there is little she can appeal to. She is not crawling or begging. She is making one offer in line with what she knows of his values. Assertive requests do not always get acquiescence; they get it more than others, but still do not get 100% positive response.

An angry parent came in to see Merran and accused her of making a laughing stock of her overweight son in the changing room. All the boys had laughed when she had commented on the fact that the boy's shorts were splitting at the seams.

Merran	Yes, I did say that unless he got some of that weight moving he would have trouble covering himself with those shorts. It was a joke.
Parent	Well, everyone found it funny except my son and I.
Merran	What would you like to happen, then?
Parent	I want you to stop picking on him just because he's bigger than the other boys.
Merran	I can assure you, I will not pick on him.

If Merran had wanted to argue with the parent and bring up the boy's laziness and lack of co-operation in PE then the matter would have escalated. And yet that is what mostly happens. Each issue must be addressed on its own and resolved in a *no blame* way. Merran can ask to see the parent about a number of issues and state them all in a *no blame* way at the appropriate time. A battle of fault-finding is not assertive. Merran values *no blame* criticism.

Merran	Mrs X, I have a problem with your son's attitude and behaviour in PE. Can we find a way round it?
Parent	(Is silent.)
Merran	His reluctance to bring his gear, his slowness in getting changed and his vanishing acts take a lot of my time. I need him to co-operate. Can you tell me how I can manage these things?

No matter what the parent's response, Merran has remained true to her values to treat everyone in an open and direct way. She looks after her own self-esteem and she enables others to do the same.

Becoming assertive is one way of lifting self-esteem. Having honourable motives, giving genuine feedback, and focusing on how criticism and praise work is one way of improving staff morale and school climate.

Feedback from people who are significant is recommended; this does not mean accepting feedback, from everyone. Asking for praise and criticism is a right but it makes one vulnerable. Assertiveness involves greater vulnerability but it gives greater life satisfaction. Remember, the navigator of a plane is only on true course for 5% of the time. The rest of the time is adjusting to the feedback given by the navigation equipment.

Exercises

1. Count how many pieces of praise and how many pieces of criticism are given over a period of time. (It has been said that we need eight hugs a day ... eight praisings to one criticism.)

2. There are two ways to view the same trait in different people, depending on your mood. Are there any on your staff?

positive	*negative*
checker	nit-picker
innovator	crank
performer	plodder
challenger	stirrer
humanizer	drop-out
driver	tyrant
harmonizer	rescuer
planner	fusspot.

3. List the initials of every member of staff and next to each put their greatest strength.

4. Prepare the compliments you can genuinely give to each member of staff.

5. Identify some criticisms you would like to give. Word them constructively.

8 Feelings and emotions

In brief

- **Feeling is an element of mind equal to cognition and will.**
  Teachers who are in touch with feelings promote cognition and will.
- **When feelings are recognized they create co-operation.**
  Teachers who deal with people on a feeling level have influence on them.
- **Feelings can be heard in the voice and seen in the body language.**
  Teachers can communicate convincingly when body language and words are complementary.
- **Feelings can be controlled by the voice.**
  Teachers can sense feelings and use the *voice* to keep calm.
- **Feelings often prevent people being assertive in practice.**
  Teachers can manager anger, anxiety and sadness and be assertive.
- **Separating feelings from actions is a key skill.**
  Teachers can identify feelings, feel them, deal with them and then debrief them without actions being destructive.
- **Feelings stored often spill at a later stage.**
  When teachers bury feelings, particularly anger and sadness, they sometimes come out at inappropriate times.

Feeling is an element of mind equal to cognition and will

Western education since the Age of Reason has valued the development of the mind, particularly the *left brain's* natural aptitudes: thinking, reasoning, logic, objectivity, sequential analysis. It has undervalued the development of the feeling, intuitive, subjective, holistic, imaginative, simultaneous synthesis of the *right brain*. The concept of *whole brain* education is still on the fringes of mainstream education.

This means that the world of the feelings is mysterious, wild, untamed and to be guarded against. *Left brain* is expected to control *right brain* by an act of will. The behaviour that arises from the right side of the brain is something to be wary of. Yet it is feeling that creates most of the action in the world. Fear, grief, hate, love and apathy overcome will and reason time and time again. Controlling these feelings until they break out or become subsumed into something else is not healthy or helpful.

Feelings recognized create co-operation

Learning about feelings gives human beings increased comfort with them. A feeling that is recognized, felt and then dealt with, with a thinking dimension added, inspires the will.

Case Study: Millie, 43, speech and drama and geography teacher

Millie was an exemplary teacher whose classes were superbly managed. Indeed she prided herself on the fact that even though the students could be difficult in other subjects, for her they were diligent, polite and even studious. They learned well and scored highly in tests. They even worked for the supplies who occasionally took classes for her, but not for supplies in other subjects.

The deputy asked her what her secret was. She said she didn't know. Sometimes they came in a bit wild and she had to settle them down, but generally that was not a problem. So the deputy decided to ask the students in her classes. Some of their comments included information on feelings.

- She knows what I'm feeling.
- When I've been stirred up she lets me have a moment to bring myself together.
- She knows when I am getting angry and she's taught me to breathe and control it.
- She tells us what she is feeling.
- She has a knack of telling me what I'm feeling and she's always right.
- When I feel gloomy she doesn't tell me to stop it, she gives me a set time to feel it.
- We talk a lot about how feelings stop us working.

- I learned from her that working can give you good feelings, rather than good results.
- I somehow feel she is on my side.
- She's a bit weird, spends time on teaching us to say 'I feel this' and 'I think that.'
- The other kids like her so I don't mess.
- She gets angry but it's not scary; it's sort of honest anger.
- She's not into punishment.
- She doesn't want any of us to have bad feelings.
- She says anger is OK as long as we tell it and don't show it.
- She hears me – feelings as well as what I say.
- Some teachers use the same words and they sound sarcastic. She doesn't.
- She always looks you in the eye when she speaks to you.

With Millie's approval, the deputy then asked three students of different ages to work together to prepare a scene which would demonstrate how this teacher, compared with another, handled an incident. They produced the following dialogue after remembering scenes from their lessons.

Class enters in usual orderly way.

Millie   Dan, your shoulders are drooping, your chin is on your chest. Do you want a desk by yourself? Right, you can have that back one by the window. Today, we will continue to make that cross-section of the ordinance survey map.

Benja   Oh, no!

Millie   Benja, you are worried that you will have the same trouble today as yesterday. Nola can come and help you because she has now come to terms with it. Who else wants a helper for the first 20 minutes? OK. At 3 o'clock I will ask each pair what they have learned from working together.

Carl   Miss, Verne isn't helping me properly.

Millie   Ah, Carl, what do you want to happen?

Carl   I want Verne to measure the road with the string because I can't.

Millie   Now Carl, perhaps Verne has other ideas. Verne, what is your idea?

Verne   Miss, I have shown him, and I want him to try for himself.

Millie   Now you two are talking to each through me. Let me hear how that sounds as a conversation between you two.

Carl   I want you to measure that road for me.

Verne   I think you are ready to do it yourself.

Carl   I think I am not.

Verne   (looking at Millie) I feel you should try and I'll watch, then if

	you can't I'll show you again.
Carl	The old feel trick!
Millie	But it works because you know the mistake is OK. Right, Carl? Benja, have you finished? Nola is feeling angry from the look on her face.
Nola	Miss, he says I have done mine wrong. Yet I was helping him.
Benja	I can do it better than her, miss.
Millie	You both feel frustrated. Can you work it out?

The deputy saw the emphasis on feeling in this scene and asked Millie about it. She had decided about four years before that most of the classes she taught didn't learn very much because they were sitting uncomfortably on feelings that they either brought into the room or created in response to one another and the school work assigned. So she experimented with a really good class and got them to tell her how they felt every time something happened. So they had to start every dialogue with her with 'I feel':

'I feel annoyed that I have to borrow the compass from Jane because we haven't enough.'
'I feel happy that there is only four minutes to lunch time.'
'I feel anxious about how much homework you have given us.'

By bringing the feelings into the open Millie learned a lot about them. She told them what she was feeling every time she spoke to them as well. Both teacher and students gave feelings a high profile and learned to respect them. She went to a drug education seminar and they were talking about how important feelings were in creating rebellious behaviour, so she read a bit about that. Then, by accident, she read an article on right and left brain attributes, and guessed that if she talked with students about how feelings and thinkings (Millie's word) were both valuable to learning, she might be able to help some of them attain better self-control. She just made it up and found it worked for her and the students too. The rule in Millie's class is that it is OK to feel any feeling, but everyone must respect others enough not to show feelings if it will disrupt them. Now, every year, Millie helps her classes to understand this and they find it useful.

The deputy was not convinced that was the whole story. The main point is that the teacher identified a problem and applied a solution which she had worked out and resourced with time, energy and expertise. She persuaded her students that feelings had a place alongside thinking in school. Too often students are offside because hormones and adolescent feelings are expected to be controlled and they have no skills for doing so. Self-control can be learned, so that the will can be used to fire learning.

Millie was open and honest with her students in the whole area of feelings. The students had a process for dealing with them that they had learned from her. She had demystified their feelings and made them acceptable in an assertive way. She had probably never heard of assertion training as a way of gaining skills with feelings. She had found her own way.

Feelings come from the inner emotions, and show in body language

Non-assertive people are usually ruled by fear, either expressed as anger and leading to aggressive behaviour, or expressed as passivity and leading to submissive behaviour. These behaviours are demonstrations of their feelings.

Submissive teachers accept too much of what they don't want from students, colleagues, seniors and authority. Their body language reflects their feelings. Shoulders are rounded, arms are limp, eyes look down; there is a whole sagging of the body posture which after the age of 40 is very visible. The voice is soft and tired-sounding and contains many *they shoulds, yes buts, if onlys*. The feelings they have in response to requests and situations they find themselves in overpower them because they think the rights of the others are more important than theirs. They either feel anxious and think they must submit or they think the other is so important that they feel cowed. Whether feeling or thinking comes first is immaterial. Low self-esteem, bad feelings and bad health, like cancer which eats away inside, result from submitting.

Too often the submissive person puts up with a feeling of being taken advantage of until an explosion occurs and then they feel justified in asserting their own needs. The martyr then makes demands. This is aggression, not assertion. Assertion does not damage anyone because it always leaves room for the other to move in line with choice.

Aggressive teachers expect others to accommodate them, and use feelings to intimidate. They expect trouble and try to defer it by getting in first with expressions of high feeling which are meant to deter any opposition. This has an effect on their body language. They tend to lean forward, often hunch their shoulders, have folded arms and a jutting chin. Their loud words are full of *you musts*, and they rarely listen. And not always are their barks worse than their bites. The feelings they have drive them to protect themselves even when protection is not necessary. The cost, on both the teacher and those receiving aggression, of constantly being on guard and attacking or defending, is too high. The bully drives people away and suffers bad health, like hypertension and strokes – they literally explode.

Every so often the aggressive one suffers tremendous guilt at their abuse of another and tries to make amends. They move into submissive mode.

Such swings take their toll on relationships at work and at home. Only occasionally is the aggressive one at work a submissive one at home, or vice versa.

It is easy to catch anger from another. In fact it is probably the most contagious of feelings. The assertive teacher has many occasions when the aggressiveness of another impinges on them and they have to resist responding in like mode.

The way out of these short-term success strategies in getting needs met is the long-term strategy of true assertiveness. In the feeling sense this simply means knowing what you are feeling, expressing it appropriately and dealing with it effectively.

Case Study: John, 33, Deputy Head, primary school

John was on the receiving end of much *virtuous* anger. Teachers, children, parents all would burst into his office and explode, venting some anger in his space. Monday morning was one such case. Bill, the second deputy, burst in.

Bill	You stupid idiot, John, you sent me off to that curriculum meeting with the wrong papers.
John	You are very angry, Bill. That meeting was important.
Bill	Too bloody right! And it is all your fault. You took them to check them and you sent me the wrong ones back. It is all your fault.
John	You may be right. I have done some stupid things at times.
Bill	Well, this time you really did it.
John	Tell me about it.
Bill	I got in there, started my presentation, took out the package to give out the details, the one I had put in my case the minute you gave it back to me, and it was the wrong one. I had none of the detail to back up my talk about truants and bullying. All I had was hot air.
John	Did they like what you had to say?
Bill	Yes, but they were sceptical. (or) No, they were dismissive of my generalizations.
John	Well, we can send them the details now. (or) What have we learned from this?
Bill	Will you or I do it? (or) That we both must double-check.

John could have said, 'You didn't check them when you put them in your case?' – and passed the blame! Bill could have said, 'I'll never trust you again.' But blaming is not an appropriate response for professionals. Too often it is easy to think that once a fault has been attributed that is the end of the matter. Covering up mistakes is not the choice assertive teachers would make, because assertive teachers know that they may not be perfect, but bits of them are excellent.

Owning-up is a most difficult task. The submissive may crumple after an initial denial, the aggressive may bombastically brazen it out, but the assertive says, 'That may be right. I may have messed it. I must in future ... .'

Feeling can be controlled by the voice

Essentially what John did was receive Bill's anger, which said 'I am angry.' John did not admit any fault, nor attribute any fault, and then he moved the exchange onto the productive ground of 'next time'. He did not return accusation for accusation, nor did his feelings match Bill's. He stayed *cool*. He might have taken the traditional deep breaths, or used some other strategy to *control* his feelings. He came from computer voice and stayed there until Bill met him in computer voice.

Eric Berne[1] identified Parent, Child and Adult voices emanating from individuals; from his work and that of his followers, seven voices are audible in transactions between people. Six of the seven voices are high in feeling and only the Adult or 'computer voice' is free of feeling. These were mentioned in Chapter 1 and can be classified as:

- Parent Critical   a voice which finds fault and is full of you's, should's and must's
- Parent Rescuing   a voice which takes responsibility from the other and is full of 'let mes'
- Parent Nurturing   a voice which teaches another and uses 'we'
- Child Rebellious   a voice which defies another with 'I won't' messages
- Child Helpless   a voice which calls for assistance with 'I can't' messages
- Child Free   a voice of jokes and fun
- Adult Computer   a voice with no feeling like a neutral gear on a car.

Asking the question 'What time is it?' receives the replies below.

[1]Berne, Eric (1968), *Games People Play*, Harmondsworth: Penguin.

- PC: Haven't you got a watch (or) can't you tell the time?
- PR: Don't worry, I'll tell you when it is time.
- PN: Oh, let's look together, see the big hand ... .
- CR: Not telling you!
- CH: I don't know either, what will we do? Oh, oh, oh!
- CF: Guess!!!!!
- AC: Two o'clock.

From this model teachers can identify the voices children, colleagues and others use on them and decide which voice they would like to respond with. Responding with a complementary voice may either establish rapport or escalate a problem, for example:

Aren't you ready yet? (PC) No, you are stopping me. (PC)
I can't get there on time. (CH) Neither can I. (CH)
I'm not giving in. (CR) Neither will I. (CR)

Responding with a crossed transaction can do the same:

You are always late. (PC) I know, please help me. (CH)
Don't expect me to help. (CR) Oh go on!!!! I'll tickle. (CF)
Let me help you with that. (PR) I don't need help. (CR)

Using the Adult Computer voice means the speaker is not going to engage in a feeling game, but is going to resolve the issue:

Where's the big hand? (CF) It is two o'clock. (AC)
Oh, you make me so mad. (PC) What makes you think that? (AC)
Bloody hell, Jane, you mucked that! (PC) I disagree. (AC)

In order to bring someone from a high feeling state so that they can communicate reasonably, it is necessary to respond from the Adult Computer voice, then move into either Parent Nurturing, which is a joint effort voice, or into a Child Free voice if a joking approach will defuse the emotion. Using these voices is an artificial way of managing feelings until a way natural to the individual emerges. The assertive person can master these voices and manage interactions on a superficial level until it becomes natural to manage the emotion.

Feelings can prevent assertiveness

What stops most people from being assertive, however, is the feeling of anxiety which is not included in the voice model of managing emotional interactions. Assertive people feel anxiety and go ahead anyway. They do not automatically go into anger or sadness. They may feel anger or sadness as well, and announce it, but they do not demonstrate it and they do not let it stop them.

Case Study: Wendy, 29, itinerant primary music teacher

Wendy had been taking music classes at three primary schools for two years. She enjoyed teaching at two of the schools but not at one of them, a school with more than its share of difficult children. One of the schools she enjoyed wanted to double her time and she wanted that. The obvious choice was to leave the difficult one. However, she dreaded telling that school that she would like to quit with them. The Head was so nice and the teachers were so relieved to get a short time off class while she did music for them.

She spent most nights for about three weeks agonizing over how she would break the news to them. She rang everyone she knew and asked if they knew of a music teacher who would like ten hours' work a week. Her life was a misery. It was almost worse than taking the difficult children. She said yes to the school that wanted more of her time and that made matters even worse. She started to have sleep problems. She was suffering from anxiety.

Finally she confessed her dilemma to a friend. The friend told her of a series of actions she could take to make it possible for her to speak with the Head of the school she wanted to leave. These actions required that she:

Believe (or act as if she believed) that

- every person has the right to ask for they want
- every person has the right to say No to any request.

Create a vision of the deed accomplished and

- do a relaxation exercise and control her breathing
- envision the conversation going the way she wanted
- hear herself saying the words she wanted to say
- feel the good feeling of success.

Reduce the anxiety she has by

- brainstorming every possible reaction of the Head to the news

- anticipating the worst that could happen when she broke the news
- anticipating the best that could happen when she broke the news
- putting herself in the shoes of that Head and imagining the responses the Head would make if she were pleased, angry, hurt, scared and indifferent to the message
- remembering a time when she had been scared and had gone ahead anyway
- remembering a good success feeling, giving it a name and doing this until the call on the name brings the good success feeling after it.

Control the anxiety on the occasion by

- dressing in clothing which gave her confidence
- assuming a confident body language
- breathing evenly
- recalling the good success feeling by naming it
- scripting the words she wanted to use and possible next lines
- feeling any anxiety that remains and going ahead despite the anxiety.

With these choices, Wendy decided she could try the breathing and brainstorm all the Head's possible responses and then do it. Over the next two days she anticipated all the responses she could, and practised some assertive sentences.

Three days later, Wendy went to the school and asked to speak to the Head at 3:30 p.m. She asked for a set time so that she could prepare herself. She went in and had the following conversation:

Wendy	Head, I will not be able to teach with you in the new year; I have extended a contract with XXX school.
Head	Oh, Wendy, I am sorry that you will not be with us, we will miss you.
Wendy	I have rung all my colleagues to see if I could find you a replacement, but I have had no success.
Head	Thank you for doing that. It was beyond the call of duty and I do appreciate it.

If the Head had said, 'Oh dear, what will we do? You must not leave us in the lurch like that' or 'We never wanted you anyway; we only had you to relieve the staff,' Wendy could have said, ' I realize you have a problem releasing staff now and I sympathize.' If the Head's reply had been 'Oh, you can't; the poor teachers need you to give them time off' or even 'Good, the children didn't enjoy music and we will spend the money elsewhere,' Wendy would have a reply ready: ' I am pleased my time has been useful to you in the past.'

Managing the anxiety that can prevent assertiveness being assimilated into daily life is a matter for feeling, cognition and will.

Separating feelings and actions is a key skill

The following is a suggested outline of a process which gives some control over feelings.

Managing your own feelings

Identify it	*Feel it*	*Colour it*
anger	heat energy	red
anxiety	shivers paralysis	black
sadness	cold limpness	blue
gladness	warmth lightness	yellow
hope	cooled excitement	green
apathy	chilled numbness	grey

State the feeling to yourself or aloud. I feel: angry, anxious, sad, glad, hopeful, indifferent.

Deal with the feeling either now or later:

> I will go away and yell and scream
> I will pretend now and go for a run later
> I will ignore it for now and come back when I am quieter
> I will cry
> I will exclaim with joy

I am stunned and will deal with it later
I need to be quiet to feel it alone
I need to talk about it
I must write about this in my journal.

Managing other people's feelings

Identify the feeling and tell them what you are receiving from them. Do this in Adult Computer voice which is feeling-free:

I see you are very angry
Your sadness is there
You are scared right now
You are anticipating the worst
You are numb with the shock.

If you are wrong, they will correct you. Recognizing the feeling makes them feel understood and tells them that you see them and where they are. Move into the feeling you want them to have – generally nurturing or free – and they may follow you.

Managing the feelings others try to impose on you

When people try to create feelings in you such as blame or guilt, respond with an Adult Computer, no feeling voice. Accept the person's feeling but not the feeling they are passing to you:

I feel your anger and I will not feel guilty about what happened
You are sad, and you blame me
You think I should feel guilty. How will that help?

These may just be words, but the words defend your feelings and give you time to choose your position. Your *buttons* are not pushed by just anyone. It is difficult to use this voice in a family situation, but not as difficult in the school environment.

Feelings are often stored and spilled later

It is usual to believe that feelings arise spontaneously. That is true. However, most people carry feelings from one situation to another and from the past into the present. When feelings are not expressed at the time of generation they are stored for later. When this happens a lot the 'bank' fills up and the feelings spill out and contaminate the present or are withdrawn to fuel a current situation. Berne[1] calls such feelings racquet (racket) feelings. Their purpose is not to be honest but to intimidate the other.

Case Study: Marty, 54, French teacher

Whenever Marty was asked to cover for an absent teacher he would go into a tirade of anguish about all he had to do and how he wouldn't be able to do this and that and if he did it he would need ... etc. He made a fuss and talked about it for days after; as a result, the deputy avoided giving him classes to cover. In fact, when he was asked to do anything that was in excess of his timetabled load, he responded with high feeling. By acting in this manner, he stalled a non-assertive deputy.

Case Study: Bindee, 33, primary teacher

Bindee was the classic angry young man. His posture was aggressive, his voice was loud, his manner was attacking, his movements were fast and pointed. He often appeared, made a heated announcement, and disappeared. He had a reputation for being difficult to handle. He was particularly sensitive to any comment about race, whether it was a simple reference to a racial custom or identification of a difference. One day he entered the staffroom and heard Claire talking to Sanjay about *The Jungle Book* by Rudyard Kipling.

Claire was saying that one of the children had brought the book to school with some large drawings of the animals that his father had done. The child wanted to show the drawings in assembly and tell the children about the story of Mowgli. Sanjay said this was OK. It was his assembly and he would find her a spot.

Bindee exploded. He accused Claire of supporting the Empire exploitation of India. He accused Sanjay of treachery and disloyalty to India. He added that they had not heard the last of this and stormed out.

This was not the time for anyone to speak with him. His feelings were too strong and this anger was too much, in fact, out of all proportion to the *offence*. Claire and Sanjay decided to forget it.

Bindee's behaviour had all the signs of transferred anger. It was as if he had a store of anger, swallowed for a long time over many issues, but triggered by any reference to race. He did not stop to judge whether any of the comments made were prejudicial to India; he automatically assumed any

[1]Berne, Eric (1968), *Games People Play*, Harmondsworth: Penguin.

reference to colonialism was racist.

Such anger can be carried by anyone and be triggered by many *harmless* references. Anger which is stored results in much body tension because a large amount of energy is needed to contain it. The 'angry young man' theme is seen throughout cultures where oppression is in the process of being lifted.

If one of Bindee's colleagues had spoken with him later about his comment, he might have dived back into the anger and been too emotional again to deal with the issue, or he might have collapsed. It would be unusual for him to carry out his threat of further action, so Claire and Sanjay were probably making a wise decision to let it go, rather than confront it. Assertive people can choose their response, because they have a strategy for managing the present – feeling control from outside themselves. By saying to themselves immediately, 'This person is very angry', instead of 'How dare he!!!!!!', teachers have an effective first strategy for managing their feelings. There is a space in which the rational left brain can have a say.

The emotional responses of others are often best accommodated by a recognition of the feeling and no confrontation at that time. When an adult is out of emotional control, containing it and dealing with it at a time when all is calm is an assertive teacher's response – not forgetting it, but dealing with it later. When the teacher is very angry and delivers an emotional outburst, then later, when calm, the teacher can talk with the receivers of the emotion and manage the aftermath, with explanation or apology.

The Head of Bindee's school may raise the matter of Bindee's display of anger at a time when it is part of a larger feedback session. On that occasion, the Head, or substitute, could speak with a no-blame purpose:

Head   I sense you are very angry and sometimes I feel your anger. It makes me uncomfortable. Is there something I can do which will allow you to describe that you are angry and yet not show it? I have noticed that you are deeply affected by any reference to race. I understand the seriousness of racist comments and will act, as you know. Not all references to anything racial are derogatory, however. Would you like to talk about that difference?

How far a senior officer's responsibility goes in detecting and addressing self-destructive behaviour is debatable. How far discussing and counselling such personal issues is a part of Human Resource Management in Education under Local Management of Schools provision will no doubt vary from school to school.

Exercises

1. Think about the emotions you most commonly feel and list them in frequency order. Put next to each the incidents, occasions, interactions that fire them.

2. List three situations where you could choose to be either mad or sad.

3. List three situations which make you anxious.

4. How would you feel if a respected colleague said each of the following? How would an assertive you respond?

   - There you are, late with your register yet again!
   - I am so angry with you!
   - Don't you ever dare interfere with my class again.
   - Oh dear, I am so disappointed in you.
   - You should be worried about what I have to say to you!

5. Identify a highly emotional request you would like to make to a significant person at school. Plan a strategy which would encourage you to go ahead with it. Check this strategy with a friend, then reflect. Can you live with the worst result? Do it!

Epilogue: A personal word

Professional dignity comes to us when we exercise our rights and fulfil our obligations with open honesty and respect for ourselves and others, no matter what behaviour is being presented.

Being assertive guarantees dignity, indeed it confers it. There are times when assertive teachers choose to behave otherwise, and accept the repercussions. Being aggressive, submissive and manipulative are short-term strategies which may be situationally efficient at the time. As general practices, however, they damage the self-image and encourage the recipient to engage in point-scoring behaviour. Assertiveness protects self-esteem and encourages others to be straight in relationships and the pursuit of goals.

When professionals accept responsibility for themselves and their actions,

- with *I* messages instead of *you* and *they* messages
- by revealing their feelings instead of demonstrating them or *baring their souls*
- by managing the feelings of others with appropriate 'voices'
- by giving criticism and praise with a real desire to be helpful instead of scoring points
- by giving criticism and praise a consideration before being influenced by it
- by being able to take a position after a realistic assessment of the *power push* needed and the amount of *co-operation* needed in the time available
- by extending to themselves, and others, the same amount of respect that they would extend to a treasured guest,

then there will be places where teachers want to be and where children see adults who are in control of themselves, coming from a place of strength.

When we look around at the people we admire, we see people who are true to themselves and respect us. They earn our respect by their behaviour towards us and others. We see their codes consistently influencing the way they behave. Such people are not the martyrs who slave selflessly for others, not workaholics who are driven by their insecurities, not manipulators who wheel and deal, trading off one for another, nor are they the bullies who dominate and bend others to their will by sheer force of personality. They are the workaphiles who operate in teams, leading and supporting in turn, and who have a variety of behaviours from which they choose the one most appropriate to the situation. Choice is possible for them because they have some ways of managing the feelings and thoughts which could drive them. They have not been born with these talents. They have learned them and they are available to all of us who will make the effort. The cost is time and effort; the reward is greater life and work satisfaction.

We all practise some of these ways of behaving at one time or another, in one place or another, or with one person or another. Increasing the number of occasions we can do so, is a challenge. Knowing we resisted a temptation to take advantage of someone or get even with someone, knowing we were skilled enough to do so, is a tremendous way of making ourselves feel good.

We can all become our own best person.

Gwynne Wilson-Brown
August 1994

Bibliography

Back, K. and Back, K. (1982) *Assertiveness at Work*, McGraw-Hill.
Berne, E. (1968) *Games People Play*, Penguin.
Berne, E. (1975) *What Do You Say After You've Said Hello*, Corgi.
Blanchard, K. (1986) *The One Minute Manager*, Willow.
Bryce, L. (1991) *The Influential Manager*, BCA.
Butler, P. E. (1981) *Self-assertion for Women*, Harper & Row.
Canfield, J. and Wells, H. (1986) *100 Ways to Enhance Self-esteem*, Prentice-Hall.
Davis, P. (1991) *Status*, BCA/Piatkus.
Dickson, A. (1982) *A Woman in Your Own Right*, Quartet.
Drummond, H. (1991) *Effective Decision Making*, Kogan Page.
Fritz, R. (1984) *The Path of Least Resistance*, Salem Stillpoint.
Gawain, S. (1986) *Living in the Light*, Whatever.
Gillen, T. (1992) *Assertiveness for Managers*, Gower.
Glasser, W. (1965) *Reality Therapy*, Harper & Row.
Glasser, W. (1969) *Schools Without Failure*, Harper & Row.
Gordon, T. (1974) *Teacher Effectiveness Training*, David McKay.
Harris, T. (1969) *I'm OK, You're OK*, Harper & Row.
Harris, T. and Harris, A. (1985) *Staying OK*, Harper & Row.
Jeffers, S. (1987) *Feel the Fear and do it Anyway*, Century.
Johnson, D. and Johnson, R. (1975) *Learning Together and Alone*, Prentice-Hall.
Keirsey, D. and Bates, M. (1984) *Please Understand Me*, Prometheus.
Laborde, G. (1983) *Influencing with Integrity*, Syntony Press.
Lynch, D. and Kordis, P. (1988) *Strategy of the Dolphin*, Hutchinson.
Mulligan, J. (1988) *The Personal Management Book*, Sphere.
Otto, R. (1986) *Teachers Under Stress*, Hill of Content.
Pease, A. (1981) *Body Language*, Sheldon.
Purkey, W. W. (1970) *Self Concept and School Achievement*, Prentice-Hall.

Roberts, T. (1975) *Four Psychologies Applied to Education*, Schenkman.
Rowe, D. (1988) *The Successful Self*, Fontane.
Scott-Peck, M. (1983) *The Road Less Travelled*, Arrow.
Sheehy, G. (1976) *Passages*, Bantam.
Sheehy, G. (1982) *Pathfinders*, Sidgwick & Jackson.
Smith, M. J. (1973) *When I Say No I Feel Guilty*, Bantam.

GOLDMINE

Finding free and low-cost resources for teaching 1993–1994

Compiled by David Brown

'It can be highly recommended because the choice of subjects, the organisation of the entries, and an index make a mass of information very easily accessible. Having used this directory to acquire resources for a couple of ad hoc topic areas, I can confidently state that it works - with ease and practicability. In the saving of teachers' time, let alone in access to materials, it really is a goldmine. I would advise any school to acquire this book. The title of the book is wholly accurate and the outlay is modest compared with the returns.' **School Librarian**

David Brown has been teaching in primary, middle and secondary schools for 23 years. It was through David's need to resource topics that he uncovered a wealth of low-cost, good quality material for use in the classroom.

GOLDMINE places these resources into topic areas, describes them and tells you where you can get them from. Since the first edition in 1985, Goldmine has developed into the country's leading directory of free and sponsored teaching resources.

Budget-conscious schools will find it saves its purchase price many times over, and parents and teachers are safe in the knowledge that all the items described have been personally evaluated by David Brown to see if they are suitable for use in the classroom. They include workbooks, leaflets, ring-binders, free videos, books, board games, full-colour posters for classroom walls, material kits (eg oils, plastics, wood etc), slide shows which can be borrowed, suggestions for visits to sites of interest, and much more!

300 pages   1 85742 099 3   £15.00

Price subject to change without notification

arena

50 POPULAR TOPICS

A resources directory for schools

Compiled by David Brown

You are resourcing a topic, and you don't know who publishes what. The school doesn't have all the publishers catalogues you need, and you don't have addresses for those you haven't got.

50 POPULAR TOPICS has been compiled to solve all these problems. The 50 most popular primary and secondary school topics are included with a huge range of books, videos, software, kits, packs, equipment and schemes for all ages between 5 and 13.

Over 2500 items from 50 suppliers are included, together with their addresses, all grouped in topics, cross-referenced in a comprehensive index and with an appendix of schemes in science, technology, geography and history.

David Brown is a schoolteacher with over 20 years teaching experience in primary, middle and secondary schools. He is also author of 'GOLDMINE', published by Arena.

1994   201 pages   Paperback   1 85742 163 9

arena

INFORMATION SOURCES FOR TEACHING

Compiled by David Brown

There are very few reference books in publication for teachers about to prepare their work. **GOLDMINE** and **The Resources Directory** begin to make some headway in that direction. Two books, however, cannot begin to address the problem faced by some teachers needing basic information about the subject they have been asked to teach. If they had the addresses of publishers, subject organisations for teachers, equipment suppliers, voluntary agencies and government organisations they would have a starting point. The present demands for improvements in teaching quality can, in part, be addressed by an increase in the amount of information available to teachers when preparing their work. This book satisfies such a need.

1995   c.270 pages   1 85742 231 7

arena

A Dictionary of Educational Terms

David Blake and Vincent Hanley

There is some confusion among governors, parents, teachers and student teachers about educational terminology, acronyms, basic features and the legal framework.

A Dictionary of Educational Terms is a convenient, easy to use book of reference to education in England and Wales, bringing together entries about the legal framework, the national curriculum and its assessment, educational organisations, and key personnel. The entries are written in a direct, jargon free style and where appropriate there is reference to other sources giving more detailed information. In the case of organisations, addresses and telephone contact numbers are provided.

1995   c.100 pages
Hbk   1 85742 256 2   Pbk   1 85742 257 0

arena